Basic Principles

OF THE

Science of Mind

Home Study Course

✳

Learn How Your Mind Can Heal You
and
Fulfill Your Deepest Desires

by

DR. FREDERICK BAILES

✳

 DEVORSS Publications

ISBN: 0-87516-404-8
Tenth Printing, 2000

DeVorss & Company, Publisher
P.O. Box 550
Marina del Rey, CA 90294-0550

For more information,
please visit our website: **www.devorss.com**

Printed in The United States of America

Man's persistent struggle
to reach his ideals is an indication
that **Something** bigger than he
is always moving within him and
encouraging him to go on in spite
of setbacks.

*

There is a **Power** within each
of us that can lift our life to its
highest level.

—Frederick Bailes

"The greatest need of the entire world today is for a quiet mind. In every stratum of society, in every town and village, the individual hungers for serenity and peace. Throughout the ages man has attempted to produce world peace by the exterior methods of force. He has failed because true peace must always arise from a genuine spirit of good will within."

Frederick Bailes

$\mathcal{K}$now the Man with $\mathcal{W}$hom You are Studying

Dr. Frederick Bailes proved the **Creative Law** of healing in his own life. Stricken by diabetes in his twenties, he was introduced to this **Law,** and made a complete recovery. That was before insulin had been discovered for the alleviation of this condition.

As a young man, he was active in the business field, and found that the same **Creative Law** that operates in physical healing can be applied to business success also.

He had been born into a family of New Zealand pioneers, and as a youth decided on a lifetime career as a medical missionary. After preparatory work, he went to England for a special course in London Missionary School of Medicine; and it was just as he was completing his training in a London hospital that he was discovered to have the so-called "incurable" condition that prevented his entering his chosen work.

He was also a graduate of Beloit College and Moody Bible Institute, and did postgraduate work at the University of Southern California. As an undergraduate, he won first prize, a gold medal, in the Wisconsin Intercollegiate Oratorical Contest. How completely he had regained his health was evidenced by his participation in sports, being captain of the undefeated Beloit College soccer football team.

For almost fifty years, he gave public lectures and taught classes on the fundamental **Laws** underlying health and prosperity. He taught special classes for various groups, including realty boards, executive clubs, and sales organizations, showing people how to apply these **Principles** on their way to success. An intensive student of Troward and Emerson, he did noteworthy work in making their somewhat abstract philosophies practical in the healing of body and affairs.

After years of lecturing across the country, he founded the Science of Mind Church in California in 1939. The following year, it affiliated with the Church of Religious Science, Los Angeles, of which Dr. Ernest Holmes was Founder and Dean. For several years, Dr. Bailes was Assistant Dean and Director of Field Activities, and he and Dr. Holmes conducted the two Sunday morning services in Los Angeles. Dr. Bailes later returned to the independent Science of Mind Church, which he had founded.

The audiences that crowded in to hear Dr. Bailes were a good cross-section of the community. In the famous Fox-Wilshire Theatre, in Beverly Hills, California, where he lectured every Sunday morning for a number of years, there were bank presidents and bank clerks; corporation presidents and their truck drivers; moving picture stars and unemployed actors; college professors and their students; barbers, manicurists, financiers, waitresses, carpenters, nurses, and housewives.

Although the theatre seated twenty-five hundred, it often filled to capacity half an hour before Dr. Bailes was to speak, and sometimes several hundred were turned away. Neither the heat of summer nor the rains of winter seemed to make much difference in attendance.

Those people came for one reason only: **They had found something that worked for them.**

Dr. Bailes made it plain that he possessed no personal "gift of healing." But he understood the **Law** of healing, and thousands have been healed as they have come to understand and apply that **Law.** Alcoholics have been healed of the desire to drink. Lonely persons have found love. Poverty has been healed by prosperity. In fact, life has been lifted to a far higher level. Here is a philosophy for living that will work for anyone who uses it.

He stressed the fact that our circumstances are always the reflection of our inner thinking, and that we must look **inside** ourselves for the real causes of our sorrows and joys.

In response to many requests from people who lived too far away to attend his classes, he put the lessons into printed form, making it possible for thousands more to study them in their homes.

"Peace in a Changing World," his highly rated broadcasts, provided daily inspiration and practical help for many years.

He is listed in **The Author's and Writer's Who's Who** (London) and in **Who's Who in California.**

Besides the Science of Mind Home Study Course, he was the author of the best-seller **Hidden Power for Human Problems, Your Mind Can Heal You,** and many booklets and articles. His books are published also in England, France, Holland, and Japan.

Contents

. . .we have reached a point where we are not only able, but also **required,** by the law of our own being, to take a more active part in our personal evolution than theretofore.   —Troward

The fact that I am here certainly shows me that the Soul had need of an organ here.   —Emerson

My Father worketh hitherto, and I work.   —Jesus

The Common Factor—the great Creative Law, or Subconscious Mind—after bringing man as far as possible through physical evolution, has now "let loose of man's hand," and man must introduce his **personal factor**—or conscious mind—to go further.
—Frederick Bailes

Introduction

> ## THERE IS A POWER WITHIN YOU
>
> It can lift your life to its highest level.
>
> It can change illness into health.
>
> It can bring peace amid turmoil.
>
> It can bring success out of failure, victory out of defeat.
>
> It can bring companionship and happiness out of loneliness.
>
> ## IT WILL RESPOND TO YOU

The above is the central theme of the Science of Mind.

These lessons will be devoted to a study of this **Power.**

We shall approach it from many different angles.

You will learn how it acts and how to **let** it work for you.

WHY SOME DESIRES ARE NOT FULFILLED

Almost everyone prays at one time or another. Why then are so many prayers unanswered? For many reasons! One is that, even as we pleaded, we held in the back of our mind all the reasons why our desires might **not** be granted. Then, when our mental blockages prevented the answer, we said something like, "Perhaps it is not God's will that I receive this answer." This is a form of blasphemy. We blamed God for what our own minds were doing.

Providence does not implant desires within us in order to mock us, but in order that they be fulfilled. The blocking of man's worthy desires is against the laws of nature.

Of that we have scientific proof. Modern psychology has repeatedly pointed out the destructive effects of such frustration on man's personality and character. Modern psychosomatic medicine says that these frustrations are the principal cause of illness.

This course will uncover the laws of answered prayer so that our desires are fulfilled by our following those laws.

LIFE IS GOVERNED BY LAWS AND PRINCIPLES

There is no favoritism in the universe. Life is not a thing of blind Fate or luck. Life is governed by laws and principles. The key to everyone's achievements is his thought, which operates by an unchanging **Law of Cause and Effect.**

Those who fail have followed the laws of failure. Those who succeed have followed the laws of success. We may fight this principle, deny it, try to evade it, but we cannot escape it. We had better face it.

For every **effect,** there is always a corresponding and adequate **cause.** We cannot plant onion seed and have roses come up. No matter how ardently we desired roses and pleaded for them, the universe could not violate its own laws out of pity for us. Just so it would be impossible for one to achieve success while the thought-pattern is of failure, or to plant morbid thoughts and expect anything but illness.

INNER CHANGE — OUTER EFFECT

The universe will give good health when we learn to build a proper health-pattern. It will give success when we learn to build a proper success-pattern. This is not done by mechanical repeating of "Every day in every way I am getting better and better." It is done by a scientific method that will unfold as we go through the lessons. It is being used today by millions of people throughout the world. These persons are getting their prayers answered. It works!

All of us have an amazing ability to change our inward patterns of thought completely. As we do this, our health and affairs change to the exact degree that we make the **inner** change. We make our own misery or happiness. Let us then never blame anyone or anything but ourselves when things go wrong. Let us look **inside** for the **cause.** We can change it. The **outer** effect will then reflect the **inward** change.

IMPLICATIONS FOR THE WORLD

The world today stands at the crossroads of civilization. It must move in one of two directions — either backward to devastating carnage and ultimate barbarism, or forward toward spiritual understanding and the highest civilization ever seen on this earth. The direction it takes is not foreordained; it is not determined by blind Fate. Man is free to go in whichever direction he **chooses.**

The students of this philosophy may well decide humanity's destiny. Starting your inquiry into the universal forces, which may be used for good or ill, you are being given a key to the future — a key that may be used to bring man out of his prison of materialism and violence into the bright light of his highest fulfillment, or which may be used to lock, with dread finality, the door that seals him into a self-chosen doom.

The issues are delicately balanced. The forces of materialism are noisy; they get the headlines. Those who are influenced by the sensational therefore think the worst is inevitable. But beneath the surface of headlined events is a movement comparable to the build-up of a great ground swell. This movement is the silent power of man's inner spiritual self.

If we believe that spiritual thought-power is an actual current of energy as real as an electric current, that it is the most tremendous force in the universe, it is reasonable to believe that the thought of our thousands of students would have tremendous impact on the world.

In taking this course, therefore, not only should you manifest the fulfillment of your personal desires, but you have become one of a spiritual family bound together in a consciousness of brotherhood beyond national boundaries, whose thought-patterns can remake the world.

A TREATMENT AND A PRAYER—HOW THEY DIFFER

Throughout this course, we use some words in a new and different way.

When people speak of prayer, they mean asking that some particular good come to them as a result of that prayer. We use a different word, one which more clearly defines the method by which we draw our good to us.

That word is "prayer-treatment" or simply "treatment." We treat for results rather than pray for them in the old manner of pleading.

A treatment is a definite movement of mind, in a definite direction, to accomplish a definite purpose. There is nothing more real and effective than a treatment intelligently given. When one treats for a result, something begins to happen beneath the surface of life that was not happening before the treatment was given.

The lessons on how to give a treatment will show the exact procedure to follow. In many instances, the words to base your own treatment on will be given. You will probably be astounded in the beginning at the very definite results that follow your treatment. These will not be miracles, but a very definite result of the **Law of Cause and Effect.**

ESSENTIAL INSTRUCTIONS FOR GETTING THE MOST OUT OF THIS COURSE

1. Know what and where the POWER is

At the outset of your studies, please make sure you understand the fundamental principle that you do not create power. You merely lay hold on that invisible **Power** that has always existed.

When we use the term **Power** or **Infinite Healing Presence,** we mean that indwelling **Wisdom** of the ages, which brought our world into being; which holds the stars in their courses and the atoms in a rock; which heals a cut finger and cements a broken bone; and which impels the tree root to seek water. Difficult to describe, its activity has been noted by the observant throughout the ages. For want of a better name, men have used the term "God," the superintending and sustaining **Intelligence** of the universe. Some use "Jehovah" or "Allah." Others use the **Infinite, Infinite Wisdom, Infinite Intelligence.** The term used is not important. What is important is that there is a **Super-Intelligence** in and through the universe and in each of us.

Cultivate the conviction that man needs nothing outside himself. Already within him is the **Infinite Healing Intelligence,** waiting to go to work.

Heretofore, you may have been unaware of this **Power.** Now, aware of it, you learn how to align yourself with it, and it does the work. As you go through the lessons, you will learn the various approaches to it, and how to apply the principle to specific areas of action.

2. Be open minded

It is imperative that the student be open minded. Truth never changes, but our understanding of it does. Newer views may sometimes appear in conflict with older beliefs, but they are not to be avoided because of this. God is still God no matter how

He is described. Faith is still faith even when expressed in scientific and modern terms, rather than in archaic language.

3. Be Intellectually honest

The key to man's freedom is his thought. If we can be courageous enough to admit that the unfortunate experiences in our lives have, in some way, been attracted by our wrong thinking, we have laid the foundation for their removal through a change in our thought. But if our pride or our stubbornness keeps us from admitting it, we thereby set in motion a law that prevents us from getting our deliverance.

4. Study

Set aside a definite time each day for a systematic plan for study of each lesson and for reading recommended books on the subject. I believe it will be most beneficial to study one lesson a week if possible, and also not to attempt to go faster the first time through the course.

Read, thoughtfully reread each lesson, underline, make notations in the margins, and use any other means that will help you to **absorb the underlying principal thoughts deeply into your consciousness.**

Keep a notebook for use with the **Special Helps in Study and Practical Application** at the end of each lesson. I recommend the standard size notebook, 8½ x 11, looseleaf.

If questions come to mind that you want to watch for answers to, write them in your notebook. Then watch, not only for the specific answer, but for every idea in any way related to it. My many years of teaching thousands of students has shown me how to anticipate questions, and I have woven the answers into the course at the time when the student is best prepared with background to grasp them.

5. Practice

We must put our lessons into practice. Without a wholehearted willingness to follow the truth you find in this course, there can be no change in your affairs. Truth never becomes **our own** until we apply it. But as surely as you put these lessons into practice, you will find new power flowing through all your affairs, and you will begin to see results.

We can begin, at this moment, to apply the truth by facing our own responsibility for what has happened to us. We can say something like this:

> Whatever situation I am in today is the direct result
> of my past thinking. I am exactly where I belong by right
> of consciousness.

True, the perfidy of others or their failure to co-operate may have contributed to my misfortune; but the accident that seemed **not** to have been my fault, or the illness that seemed **not** to come through any fault of mine, was made possible by the general tendency of my thought. This, in some way, attracted to me these persons or these events or things that have happened to me even while I was longing for, praying for, and trying to get their very opposites.

The **Special Helps . . . in Practical Application** at the end of each lesson will give you further specific help in practicing what you learn.

The human consciousness must be changed to a God-consciousness, which carries in itself all fulfillment. The success of this course for you lies in your changing a consciousness that has brought you experiences you do not like into a consciousness that will bring you your most cherished desires.

This is not realized by mastering a succession of facts. It comes through a changed feeling, a changed belief, which finally becomes a warm inward conviction. This latter is what is called **knowing the truth.**

Finally, to you, the student of this course, who are now a part of this, the greatest dynamic on earth, I say, "Do not work at your studies tensely with a straining for results. Just **let** the silent **Power** of the **Infinite Healing Presence** flow through you, healing mind, body, and affairs, and out into the world healing its ills also."

You have my best wishes as you do so.

Frederick Bailes

Lesson 1

YOUR MIND AND HOW IT WORKS

MIND HAS SURFACE AND DEPTHS

Two phases of one mind

Surface mind

— the power to choose

Deeper mind
— the creator of our experiences
— the maintainer of the body
— the storehouse of experience
— the obedient giant within us
— the loom that weaves thought into thing

CAUSE AND EFFECT

The universe is fair
Thoughts are seeds in the creative soil of **mind**
The problem of evil

THE IMPORTANCE OF CHOICE

INFINITE MIND

INFINITE WISDOM

Central dynamic of all religious philosophies
The WISDOM is the POWER

HEALING — WHAT IT IS

1

FIRST LESSON
GOALS

To understand:

The important difference in the functions
of the two phases of your mind

How the **Law of Cause and Effect** operates in our lives

What we mean by **Infinite Mind**

Where the real healing lies

To make a definite beginning in the practical
application of what you have learned

Our thoughts are the only tools with which we work. Our mind is the only area in which we produce results. But our physical conditions and our other experiences are the places where we **see the results** produced by the tools of our thought through the Science of Mind.

Every one of us wishes to bring into his life something that is not there today. You can bring that good experience into your life. Anyone can draw the good things of life to himself once he understands the inner workings of his own mind, just as anyone can swim across a pool once he learns the laws of swimming.

MIND HAS SURFACE AND DEPTHS

Suppose we think of the mind as though it were an ocean. The ocean has a surface, and it has depths. Man sailing on the surface can see what floats there in the way of flotsam and jetsam. He can map the surface showing the ocean's fingers reaching into the bays and inlets. He is familiar with its surface calms and the rough water whipped up by storms.

But beneath the surface are the vast impenetrable depths, full of mystery. Once called unfathomable, they go down in places for miles. We do not see the great swarming mass of living forms that swim there. No one can tell where the surface ends and the depths begin, for there is no rigidly marked dividing line. Oceanographers tell us that the storms whip up only a comparatively few fathoms of the surface; while far beneath, the great depths lie undisturbed and still except for sub-surface currents that flow silently.

The terms "surface" and "depths" are used only for the purposes of description, for the ocean is all one mass of water. It is an indivisible **one.**

Like the ocean, the human mind is all **one;** yet two distinctly different types of activities are carried on within it.

The failure to grasp the difference in these two types of activities causes the confusion, unhappiness, illness, and poverty in the lives of those who do not get what they want from life.

On the other hand, the understanding of this difference and the application of that understanding bring healing and prosperity. As the student learns this difference, he moves away from the place where he is defeating himself to the place where he is working in harmony with his deeper nature, thus getting what he wants from life.

This course teaches the important difference between the ways **surface mind** and **deeper mind** work.

Two phases of one mind

The student must clearly remember that there are not two minds, but two phases of one mind, or two spheres of activity in which his mind operates in two different ways.

The psychologist uses different terms for these two phases of our minds. I mention them in passing so the student will recognize them when reading the literature of psychology. But it is better to stay with my terms of **surface** and **deeper** for a simpler understanding.

What the psychologist calls "objective" or "conscious" mind is called **surface mind** throughout this course. What he calls "subconscious," "subjective," or "unconscious" mind, is called **deeper mind.**

surface mind	**deeper mind**
conscious mind	subconscious mind
objective mind	subjective mind
	unconscious mind

Each phase has a specialized manner of working.

Surface mind

We use **surface mind** when getting a telephone number. We consciously think of each digit before dialing it. When one learns to play the piano, **surface mind** consciously directs the playing of each note until, through repetition, one has become so familiar with piano technique that individual finger movements have passed into **deeper mind,** leaving the **surface** phase free for reading the score and, if desired, words of a song that the performer wants to sing, or even for carrying on a conversation.

— the power to choose

Surface mind can, therefore, be called "directing" mind.

It is characterized by the words "I choose." With it, we weigh values; we weigh reasons for and against; we judge; we decide; we deliberately **choose** what we want to do, what we want to be, what we want to have. And we deliberately **choose** the **thoughts** we want to think.

All our **choices** are made in **surface mind.**

"I choose" is a key phrase throughout this course. Please keep it clearly in mind.

Deeper mind

How deep is our mind? Far, far deeper than most of us think. We shall say more of that later. For now, we are concerned with what it does for us.

— the creator of our experiences

Deeper mind is the creating, the manufacturing, phase of mind that takes what **surface mind** gives it and turns thoughts into things. Beneath the surface, it works ceaselessly to turn those thoughts — both good and bad — into the outward conditions of our lives.

It has no power of choice. It never reasons. It cannot refuse to take what **surface mind** gives it. It must always work from a pattern, and it has no choice but to work from the pattern of thought that comes to it from **surface mind.** Like the soil that must accept any seed, it must accept any thought.

Deeper mind is habitual mind. Whatever we entertain often enough and vividly enough in our **surface mind** — whether by conscious, deliberate **choice** or by choice made so rapidly that we are not aware we have made it — eventually passes into **deeper mind,** where it continues to act automatically. This is the process by which we learn everything that we learn.

A negative disposition, for instance, is the result of repeated negative thoughts that have sunk into **deeper mind** and have become habitual. But a cheerful, happy disposition can become just as automatic by conscious **choice** of positive thoughts. Thus it is not true that some people are blessed with positive natures, and others cursed with the opposite. People are not born optimistic or pessimistic; they learn to be what they are.

What anyone earnestly desires to be, he may become, not, however, by waving a magic wand but by the same procedure he uses to learn to play the piano or to swim.

Deeper mind is the most reliable agent in the world for bringing **choice** into form. We can raise the level of the thought of **deeper mind** by using the power of conscious deliberate **choice** that we have in **surface mind.**

It is the level of the thought of **deeper mind** — of our inward mental states — that makes us and our outer circumstances what they are and will become. **Deeper mind** has access to infinite resources. It knows how to heal any condition, effortlessly. To it there is no big, little, hard, easy.

All healing — whether of body or affairs — all success, all prosperity, all mastery over destructive habits, **is produced within deeper mind before appearing in outer manifestation.** This is a fundamental tenet of our belief.

Nothing goes on anywhere in the universe without a preceding action of Mind sometime, somewhere.

— the maintainer of the body

Who knows how to beat his own heart? **Deeper mind** knows, and is keeping our heart beating, our lungs breathing, our food digesting — all without any conscious effort of **surface mind.** It is contracting and expanding muscles so we can dial the telephone,

5

play the piano, walk across the room, and do whatever else our **surface mind chooses** to do. It is carrying on all the many and varied complex activities within our body that the **surface mind** of most people does not even know about, much less know how to do.

— the storehouse of experience

A person may have a conscious experience today; tomorrow or next year he will have "forgotten" it. Yet it has not gone out of existence; it has passed from his **surface mind** down into his **deeper mind,** where it is stored for future reference. Every experience through which we have ever passed is thus stored away.

What we call "memory," or "recollection," is merely the call of the **surface mind** for something that has been stored in **deeper mind.** This complex and mysterious interaction of the two results in past experiences being yielded up for present use.

Thought is an active thing, never still, always trying to find an outlet in some form. Each thought retains its own distinctive character and can work only according to its own nature.

Negative, destructive thoughts continue to work negatively beneath the surface, and in due time will yield up some outer experience that corresponds to them. We may have long forgotten the storing of the thought, and are, therefore, surprised when we find troublesome things happening to us. There is nothing mysterious or unfair about this. We are not being singled out by Fate for its buffetings. We are only reaping what we have sown sometime, somewhere. This does not mean that our past wrong thoughts need bother us forever. We can neutralize them by deliberate **choice** of the good.

In like manner, every positive, constructive thought seeks to find an outlet. Nothing is ever wasted. Those for whom we did some kindness may seem unappreciative; our motives may have been questioned or misunderstood even though we gave up some advantage in order to do the kind thing. But the law of one's own thought continues to operate regardless of others' reaction; and sometime, perhaps long after we have forgotten it, that kindness will yield its fruit in some windfall of happiness, perhaps from a totally different quarter.

Deeper mind is the storehouse of the experience of the race. It carries all racial knowledge in its memory. It knows how every successful business was ever built, how every sale was ever made, how every alcoholic was ever freed, how every mate was ever brought to the loved one. It knows all this because it itself brought all those blessed things to pass. It knows how to bring every physical healing, for it is one with **Infinite Mind.**

6

— the obedient giant within us

Deeper mind is characterized by complete, unswerving **obedience** to **surface mind.** It has no power to choose; it can only **obey.** All its vast knowledge and creative **Power** are dedicated to the person who learns how to use it.

When, as a very small boy in New Zealand, I was visiting an uncle who lived on a farm, he put me up on one of his huge work horses, gave me the reins, and told me how to start the horse and turn him in the direction I wanted to go. The powerful animal **obediently** moved off in the direction I **chose.** All that power was at the command of my small self. He was perfectly willing to do what I wanted him to do. He knew only to **obey.**

The vast creative force operating in our **deeper mind** is willing to make us whole. It knows only to **obey.**

— the loom that weaves thought into thing

We all know enough about the principles of rug-weaving to know that there are a loom, threads, a weaver (or overseer) — and a rug.

The loom has only one task; that is, to keep weaving. It does not decide whether it will weave a beautiful or an ugly rug. Hour after hour, it moves back and forth, while yard after yard of rug comes slowly forth at the end of the loom.

The weaver watching it may be displeased and outraged by what he sees coming out, but he does not berate the loom and say, "Why have you done this to me?" He does not sit at the other end crying over the ugly pattern wishing it would somehow change into a thing of beauty. He knows that the only place where beauty can be made to replace ugliness is on the rack of spools at his end before the **obedient** weaving apparatus gets it, and so he changes the threads. He takes off a dark spool, replacing it with a brighter color; he exchanges a gaudy yellow for a mellow gold. Then he starts the machine once more, and as he watches what now comes out at the other end, he is pleased.

The loom, however, doesn't care. It is impersonal. It has no choice but to weave whatever threads are given it, and it does so according to the pattern set by the weaver. The weaver is responsible for the result.

Daily, man's **loom of mind** weaves the pattern of his life. If he does not like the pattern, he is foolish to sit crying about it or wishing it would change. He is wrong to complain about "luck," or to berate "Providence." He, and he alone, is the weaver.

Using intelligence, he must alter his threads of thought by changing his harsh, critical attitudes for more kindly, tolerant ones. He must cease his hidden hostilities; he must stop thinking that the world is against him. He must remove from his mind the ugly green of envy and grudges, the dingy black of pessimism. He must banish thoughts of lack and limitation, replacing them with the expectancy of good. He must cease his morbid thoughts about illness being forced upon him without his consent. He must cultivate the quiet assurance of an **Infinite Healing Presence** within. All these and many more thought-patterns we shall discuss as the course progresses.

In this first lesson, I want the student to gain the conviction that his **deeper mind** is the loom that momentarily weaves the threads of his thought into the stuff of his outer world, and that the loom is always completely dependable, never dropping a thread of thought, but ceaselessly weaving what he gives it. Just so long as he gives it beautiful, constructive thoughts, it is his friend, who fabricates for him, in the depths of his **inner** world, that which is beautiful and constructive in his **outer** world. If his thoughts are otherwise, the result will be otherwise, for the **loom of mind** "does unto us as we believe."

By now, it must be apparent to the student that, while man's mind is one and indivisible, it has two interacting phases, which, for the purpose of study, we take up separately. And if I seem repetitious, it is because my fifty years' teaching of this subject has revealed that those students succeed best who learn clearly to separate the activities and characteristics of the two levels of mind.

Deeper mind is the **working, producing** phase of mind, while **surface mind** is the **choosing, selecting** phase of mind. **Surface mind chooses** what shall come into the life, but is helpless to produce it. **Deeper mind** is the only agent in the universe that can bring that choice into manifestation.

CAUSE AND EFFECT

The great **Law of Cause and Effect** gives back to us what we have put in.

The universe is fair

Life never lets us down; we let ourselves down. Life never fails us; we fail it. Life is a part of **Cause and Effect; Cause and Effect** is likewise part of life, the greatest ally one could ever have. But we have so filled our thought with the gloomy, the destructive, that we have failed to give the **loom** the sort of materials with which it could weave a desirable pattern.

Thoughts are seeds in the creative soil of mind

Man is sowing seeds of thought every time he thinks. Buried beneath the soil of mind, the good and the bad seeds are indwelt by the same **Principle of Life.** They grow silently together, like the tares and the wheat, until the harvest.

Some come to harvest-time one year, some another, but eventually all man's thoughts appear in some form in his life.

This will explain why we said in our Introduction that each of us, at any moment, is exactly where he belongs by right of consciousness. There is no "fate" but our sowings; there is no "destiny" but our choices; there are no "bad breaks" or "bad luck" but the silent unfolding from the **deeper mind** of what we planted foolishly and in our ignorance.

In this course, we shall learn to plant wisely, according to the true Science of Mind.

An understanding of this will enable us to wipe out self-pity and complaint, for it places squarely on our own doorstep both the causes of our unhappiness and the beginning of our happiness. Moreover, it removes the seething resentments that poison the lives of many persons, for it makes plain that others could never hurt us unless we first had prepared the soil and planted the seeds.

Naturally, they are culpable because of their unkindnesses, but the circling **Law of Cause and Effect** will quite impersonally bring into their lives the results of their own **choices.** This is why a wise student of mind once said, "Dearly beloved, avenge not yourselves . . . . Vengeance is mine; I will repay . . . saith the Lord [Law]."

The problem of evil

Here it might be well to point out that the Bible is made more understandable and reasonable when one understands a certain principle of interpretation, which is this: the word "Law" can often be substituted for "Lord." God is not vengeful, but the impersonal **Law of Cause and Effect** produces what looks like vengeance. It does not do it with intent to punish, however, any more than the river punishes with drowning the person who falls into it before he has learned to swim. The river will drown him without hating him. On the other hand, if he has learned to swim, it will, without loving him, buoy him up as he makes for shore. In both cases, it is utterly impersonal.

The **Law of Cause and Effect** is equally impersonal. It will produce illness or health, poverty or plenty, happiness or unhappiness, with the same completeness. When the Bible says in effect, "I am the Lord; I create good and I create evil," those who have not understood the interchangeability of "Lord" and "Law" have said, "How can it be that a God of love creates evil also?"

The answer is that the Law (Lord) is the automatic bringer of man's thought into form. If man's thought is evil, "I the Law"

9

creates it into evil. If his thought is good, "I the Law" creates it into good. This is the universal **Law of Cause and Effect,** which is the only way in which the **Infinite Intelligence** works.

THE IMPORTANCE OF CHOICE

Nothing is ever forced upon us without our consent. Every moment we live, we are **choosing** something. Often our **choices** are made so rapidly that we are not conscious of the process of **choice,** but, nevertheless, it is there.

For example, when we say, "Three times three is nine," there are a great many lightninglike **choices** that come before this conclusion. We must decide that it is not six, eight, five, or some other number. A child, unfamiliar with multiplication, might hit on any other number.

We who attended school under the older system recall the deadly monotony of daily repeating in unison, "Two and two are four. Three and three are six." This was a process of training in **choice,** whereby we rejected the wrong answers and **chose** the correct one. After a time, these correct answers became automatic with us, because they had dropped into **deeper mind,** which released them on demand.

Anything that is repeatedly **chosen** by **surface mind** is eventually stored in **deeper mind.** Though it may sometimes be difficult to recall, **deeper mind** never forgets anything that **surface mind** has released to it in order to focus on something else.

Our power of **choice** is the greatest blessing we have, for with it comes the ability to select the kind of mental states we entertain and hence our experiences. The encouraging feature of what appears a discouraging problem is that as we change our inner mental state, our outer experiences will change in conformity to it. To the extent that we learn to control our mental states, we control our lives.

I cannot emphasize often enough the extremely great importance of "I choose." Cultivate conscious, deliberate **choice.**

To sum it up again, **surface mind** sees, evaluates, and **chooses** what shall go to **deeper mind,** which takes the material given it and weaves it into the outer pattern of man's life. **Deeper mind** possesses amazing power to bring our good to us.

INFINITE MIND

Deeper mind is the fabricating, or constructing, **power** that lies within man, but it is by no means all of that **Power;** it is only that part of the great **Infinite Intelligence** that continually streams through man. This **Infinite Intelligence** shows itself as a **Wisdom** manifesting not only within man but throughout the universe.

INFINITE WISDOM

The activity of **Wisdom** is seen in the orderly march of the planets around the sun, in the movement of other tremendous galaxies around other vaster centers, in the confluence of great currents of energy that stream from hidden centers throughout interstellar space. We know the atom to be a miniature solar system. We find a curious mathematical exactness in the structure of crystals and cells. We see a **Wisdom** that knows how to build a perfect human body in approximately nine months, fully equipped to start its earthly life-cycle, even though the mother hasn't the slightest idea of the way to build a single cell in that child.

This **Wisdom** lies deep in the mental make-up of every soul born into the world. It knows how to keep the heart beating with mathematical regularity. It heals a cut by a mysterious chemical process that man does not know how to duplicate. It heals broken bones by arranging for the outpouring of a "bone-cement" that welds the broken ends together. The doctor merely "sets" the bone; the **Infinite Wisdom** welds it together.

All this speaks to us of an **All-Knowing Thinker** behind the universe, and operating through the universe. Observant men of all ages have noticed it. Some have called it **Universal Intelligence,** an impersonal name. Others have used the term "God," personal in a broad sense. In the Science of Mind, it is usually called the **Infinite Wisdom** or the **Infinite Healing Presence.**

One of the purposes of this course, if not the chief purpose, is to study the nature of this **Wisdom** and the ways in which man can co-operate with it for the healing of any sort of wrong action in body or environment. **It is the power within you.**

In later lessons, definite techniques will be presented, and the student will find that he need have no superstitious awe in approaching **Infinite Wisdom,** for its action is as definite and as natural as the action of electricity or of aerodynamics. When one learns how to align himself with its working principles, he can draw into his life those things that he formerly thought to be accessible only to "luckier" persons.

Central dynamic of all religious philosophies

The **Wisdom,** or **Infinite Healing Presence,** is broader than any sectarian system, and none has any monopoly on it. Under whatever name it appears, it is the central dynamic of any abiding religion. Any religion that has ever altered men's lives, from ancient times down to our myriad Christian sects, has done it through the power of **Infinite Wisdom.** It is the living center around which creed, form, ritual, and ceremony of all sorts have been built. It is the working heart; the latter are the outer trap-

11

pings. It is the fundamental without which there can be no true religion; the latter may be selected according to the preference of the individual.

Without the **Infinite Wisdom,** any so-called religion is a mere system of ethics, furnishing no dynamic that will enable the adherent to attain mastery over himself or his environment.

The Science of Mind is primarily a philosophy of life that fits within the framework of any and all religions. We do not ask our students to leave their churches; they will be better members of these for having a clearer understanding of the **power** within them.

The WISDOM is the POWER

All great spiritual leaders, ancient and modern, have had a deep sense of the nearness and availability of the **Infinite Healing Wisdom.** These men would not have become great spiritual leaders had they not found this secret of power; they would have been merely advocates of a beautiful system of ethics dangled before men, tantalizing them with some highly desirable ideal that they were powerless to reach. But testifying to their knowledge of the **Wisdom** within were the "signs and wonders" that followed their work.

It is a striking fact that whenever a person has come to see clearly the tremendous power of the Infinite Healing Presence, that person has been able to speak his word for the healing of conditions.

HEALING — WHAT IT IS

In this course, we do not speak of "curing" but of "healing." The reason is that "heal' means "make whole." The person torn apart by his fears, hates, or greeds is not a whole person. He is a circle with one or more segments missing.

Healing is, first of all, something that happens at a person's real center — in his thought-life.

This reintegration, or making whole, then spreads out through his **outer** physical affairs in what the materialist calls healing, but which is only the **outer** fruit of an **inner** central healing. The **outer** bodily or financial manifestation is only the shadow thrown on the **outer** screen of one's affairs by the healing, or making whole, of the **inner** man.

The healing, then, is the healing of the false **inward** belief; the manifestation in form of this changed belief is the **outer** healing, fruit of the new belief.

Quite naturally, one is delighted at this manifestation, for we are all human enough to desire physical betterment; but here, in this first lesson, the student is warned that he must know where the real healing takes place; otherwise, he will find himself treating conditions instead of **causes.**

For example, in the Sermon on the Mount, the Great Teacher was trying to show the people the **inner,** hidden **Principle** of wealth, but they had their minds set on physical money, which is only the **outer** token. This led Him to give utterance to the basic **Principle**: "Seek ye **first** the Kingdom of God and His righteousness [right thinking] and all these things shall [as the natural sequence] be added unto you." Prosperity is not primarily money; it is a deep **inward** state of mind out of which money grows.

The person who catches only a little of the Science of Mind is likely to fall into the error of thinking that all he has to do is to "think" of health or prosperity and it will be his. We wish that were so, but unfortunately — or fortunately — it is not. Millions of persons "think" on these things; yet nothing happens to change their condition. We must learn the techniques through which we release this tremendous **power** within us, for it is the creator of wealth.

The difference between the beginner and the skilled user of the Science of Mind is the difference between the surface swimmer and the scuba diver. One plays around on the surface; the other searches the depths using the added power of his extra equipment.

In Lesson 2, we shall have some very definite ways to help you change your thinking to what you want it to be. We shall also take up the first foundations of how to treat so you are able to get results.

SPECIAL HELPS IN STUDY
AND PRACTICAL APPLICATION

These special helps have been carefully prepared to help you get the most out of this course.

Questions on the lesson

A series of questions enables the student to get a complete picture of the material studied. You will find the questions highly valuable in uncovering concepts you might otherwise pass by.

I advise that you first study the lesson carefully, then put it aside, write the answers to the questions, and, finally, **check your answers by the lesson.**

Keep the answers as a running commentary on the course **for your own benefit.** At its conclusion, you will find they have become a record of your own growth in consciousness.

1.   Name and explain the two phases of man's mind, giving the chief characteristics of each.

2.   Where do our thoughts go after we have thought them?

3.   What is the explanation for unexpected happenings, both pleasant and unpleasant, in our lives?

4. Think of illustrations other than that of the loom to show the impersonalness and exactness of **deeper mind** as it creates thoughts into things.

5.   Think of illustrations of the **Law of Cause and Effect** in the material world.

6.   Why do we say that we are where we are by right of consciousness?

7.   Why is choice so important?

8.   What are some of the names by which **Infinite Wisdom** is known?

9.   Why do we prefer to use the term "heal" rather than "cure"?

10.   Where does the real healing take place?

Collateral reading suggestions

I like to encourage wide reading, for it gives deeper insight and thus greater depth to our understanding and a firmer foundation for our belief.

Different authors use different approaches, and the same author may at times use a different one. These can work together to bring the student more surely to his destination — to know the truth.

The first time through the course, a few students may find it not possible to do any of the collateral reading. Some will do all of it. It is my desire that all of you will eventually do all of it. I strongly recommend that you do.

Inquire at your public library or local bookdealers for the books.

Frederick Bailes: Hidden Power for Human Problems
                         Introduction and Chapter I
                  "What Is This Power That Heals?"
                  Your Mind Can Heal You, Chapter III

Emmet Fox: The Sermon on the Mount, Chapter III

Practical application

Begin now to use this **Principle.**

. . . thought-training

Watch for evidences, familiar and unfamiliar, of **Wisdom** at work in trees, stars, animals, and remind yourself that this same **Wisdom** is working in your body and affairs.

. . . writing suggestion

Make a list of the conditions in your life that you wish to eliminate and of the new conditions that you wish to bring in.

Take an impersonal look at your thoughts and actions, and make a list of those that you think should be dropped and those that should be cultivated.

Do you see any relationship between the lists?

. . . treatment for a particular experience

Select some one thing, perhaps more, but at least one thing that you desire to see manifested before the end of the course. You might write it down to make it definite. After you have selected it, say quietly to yourself:

This experience exists **now** for me in the **Infinite Mind.** Each day I grow in understanding of the supreme **Law,** which brings it forward into manifestation. I do not try to force it. I **let** it come forth through my awakening consciousness, and give thanks for it even before I see it in form.

. . . treatment for general good

I face the future with happy expectancy, with wonder.

I wonder what new experiences of the good, the joyous, the enriching, lie in wait for me.

I wonder what new persons will be drawn into my life, what new stores of health and vitality will be opened, what new depths of understanding will be uncovered within me.

The future lies before me, "stretched in smiling repose."

It is an unmarked, unmarred page.

My thought is my pen, and life is what I write.

No one else can write upon that page.

I therefore **choose** to know this day that the experiences that lie before me will be the best I have ever known.

And it **is** so.

Lesson 2

THOUGHT
AND ITS POWER

WHY OUR THOUGHT HAS POWER

MATERIALISTIC versus SPIRITUAL THINKING

THOUGHTS BECOME THINGS
Man's highest thought

WHAT CAN WE KNOW OF GOD?
God is ORDER
God is HARMONY
God is POWER
God is WISDOM
God is LOVE

MAN REPRODUCES THE INFINITE NATURE

TREATMENT — A TURNING TO PERFECTION
Treating for health
Treating for prosperity

ELIMINATE NEGATIVE SPEECH
Watch your words
Handle negative experience in a positive way

EVERY EFFECT HAS AN ADEQUATE CAUSE
Look within for causes

NEW MENTAL HABITS CAN BE FORMED

SECOND LESSON
GOALS

To understand:

    Why our thought has power

    What spiritual thinking is

    The first fundamental for successful treatment

To take a definite step in eliminating

    negative speech

A beginning student often says, "Wouldn't it be presumptuous of me to think that **my** thought has such tremendous penetrating power that it could actually make alterations in the tissues of the body, and thus induce healing?" It would. Or, "Doesn't it seem ridiculous that a mere change in my way of thinking could increase my sales or gain a promotion or increase my salary?" It does.

But his questions show that he does not yet understand the **Creative Process.** Perhaps the following illustration will show what we mean.

WHY OUR THOUGHT HAS POWER

The individual might be likened to an electric light bulb. The light manifests through it, but is **not** produced by it. Far back in the mountains are great lakes held back by giant dams. The lake water is diverted so as to run over turbine blades which are so tied in with generators that electricity is produced. This electricity, conducted through high tension wires, passes through transformers which step it down until it can pass through ordinary house wires. Thus it is led from the power-source into the tiniest wire of all, the wire within the light bulb. It cannot be contained within this tiny wire; and so, to describe the process somewhat roughly and unscientifically, the electric power bursts forth into light inside the bulb.

The little bulb would, indeed, be presumptuous to say, "Look what I am doing!" Yet it is well to remember that all the tremendous reserve of electricity would be useless for lighting without that tiny bulb. It is the interaction of the two that produces the result.

The Infinite Healing Presence is a surging **Power.** In a co-operative movement, it finds outlet through an ordinary person. Each needs the other, and there must be tight connections between them. Just as there may be plenty of electricity flowing along the wires, but, because of imperfect connections, no light, so the degree of oneness between the healing **Source** and the individual determines the extent of the manifestation.

When the Great Teacher said, "I and the Father are one," he evidently referred to this close connection, which explains the almost perfect flow of **Infinite Power** through him. The degree to which the student can bring himself to think in agreement with the **Infinite** thinking will determine the power that accompanies his word.

So it is not man's thought **of itself** that produces the results. Man's thinking becomes the vehicle for the **Creative Power** to flow through. Man's **mind** is the wire along which **Power** flows from **Power-Source** to electric bulb.

MATERIALISTIC versus SPIRITUAL THINKING

At this point, we should begin to understand the meaning of spiritual thinking. This does not mean "goody-goody" or sancti-monious thinking. It does not necessarily have to do with church attendance or Bible reading, although both of these exercises are desirable as aids in cultivating a higher consciousness; a person may never enter a church yet be a deeply spiritual thinker.

Spiritual thinking is that method of thought that brushes aside the surface, physical, apparent interpretation of things, and sees into the spiritual **Reality** beneath.

Materialistic thinking is occupied with what it can see, taste, smell, hear, and handle. It accepts only that which can be mathe-matically demonstrated, or proved, in the laboratory. God has never been seen; His existence cannot be proved; therefore, the materialist makes the mistake of ignoring the existence of a silent, effortless, unseen **Power** that acts from within him.

The spiritual thinker, however, has had experiences within the depth of his own inner self. These inner communings cannot be demonstrated in the laboratory; yet they have brought him certain states of peace, perhaps mastery over his lesser self. He therefore rightly believes that he has established some sort of contact with **Something** or **Someone** beyond it all.

The materialist believes in the surgeon's knife, but not in the spiritual union with the **Source** of all healing. He can see the one, but for him the other may not exist. Many materialists have high, unselfish ideals, but materialism carried to its logical ulti-mate would draw man back to the level of the animal, for if life has no spiritual values that endure into our unseen life beyond the grave, man's smartest philosophy would be a dead-end street.

There is the person who says, "Look out for yourself. Do the other fellow before he does you. Money is your only friend. They won't ask you how you got it, but they'll look up to you if you have it. Ideals are all right to talk about, but this is a dog-eat-dog world, and you had better get in the first bite."

The spiritual thinker places a higher value on ideals (unseen) than on material advantage (seen). He may be, and often is, a highly successful, rich businessman; but he places a much higher value on honor, integrity, his given word, truth, and fair dealing than on his material success.

We do not lose sight of the fact that the line of division be-tween the two categories is not always as definite as I have made it, but I have drawn the picture of the two types in order to make the distinction clear.

THOUGHTS BECOME THINGS

One of the fundamentals of the Science of Mind is this:

Man's inner world of thought is translated into his outer world of things.

There is no inner yardstick to measure the quality, depth, or height of man's thinking; but as water cannot rise higher than its source, man's world of affairs can rise no higher than its inner source. It follows that the higher the quality of the thought, the higher will be the manifestation.

Man's highest thought

What then is the highest thought of which man is capable?

The answer must be that his loftiest thought is that which is concerned with the ideals we have just mentioned and the even higher thoughts that center themselves on the spiritual, on God, on the **Intelligence** that obviously lies within all nature, breathing through it. But what do we, or can we, know about such a **Supreme Intelligence?**

WHAT CAN WE KNOW OF GOD?

In the first place, no one has ever seen God. All we can do is to deduce something about the nature of the **Infinite** by watching closely the signs of His (or Its) handiwork. We are all impressed by the beauty of a sunset, of an orchid, or of the cool serenity of the moon on a cloudless night. But these might be only subjective impressions that may not disclose anything about the nature of the **Infinite.**

The persons who should be able to tell us more are the scientists who have spent a lifetime delving into the mysteries of nature. These men have roamed outer space through giant telescopes, peered into the heart of the atom through microscopes, and cut deep into living tissue to probe the mysteries of circulation. They have dissected the cell to learn the exact number of chromosomes in the different living species, and have gone into the brain to dissect the way nerve energy flows. They have studied the composition, weight, and speed of those immense worlds that are only pinpoints of light in the sky.

God is ORDER

These men, almost without exception, have spoken of the marvelous order and regularity revealed by their studies, and of the mathematical exactness with which everything seems to be put together. They have declared that **Order** seems to be one of the first **Laws** of the universe.

God is HARMONY

Pythagoras startled the ancient world by declaring that the heavenly spheres move upon each other with such well-ordered precision that they throw off a very faint music, which he called "the music of the spheres," and which we would call **Infinite Harmony.** This, he said, is too faint to be heard by those who are engrossed and absorbed in the material. Since then, many other scientists have hinted at a celestial **Harmony** that is the outgrowth of the **Order** of the universe.

God is POWER

Power needs no argument. It is evident that tremendous currents of **Power** operate to keep the entire universe of suns, stars, and planets on their courses.

God is WISDOM

Wisdom has already been mentioned. The wisdom that guides a root to seek nutriment, which enables the flower or the tree to maintain life and grow, must be God-**Wisdom** since it cannot lie in the root itself. The wisdom that enables the heart to beat regularly, the cells to select the proper nutritive elements from the blood, the wisdom that guides the processes of digestion, the marvelous chemistry of the endocrine glands which assembles simple materials from food substances, and combines them into complex hormones — this is God-**Wisdom.**

God is LOVE

And what shall be said of **Love?** God is **Love;** yet we cannot imagine the **Infinite** to be softly sentimental in any maudlin manner. Love is a sincere well-wishing for another, which provides the means for the greatest growth and expansion of the beloved. This the **Infinite** quite evidently has, for the **Love** of God is evidenced in every law, every power, every attribute that man finds within himself or at his disposal, enabling him to "rise upon the steppingstones of his dead self to higher things."

Man makes a mistake when he thinks that the only love is that easygoing fondness that gives in to another person's pleading even when his better judgment tells him that his indulgence will not benefit the one concerned. True love is sometimes shown by its ability to say no.

These, then, are some of the qualities and characteristics of the **Infinite** that are based upon reasonable assumptions. There are others, as **Life, Beauty, Self-Sufficiency, Light, Holiness (Wholeness), Justice,** which can be deduced by the student through careful, logical thinking. Those we have stressed are sufficient for the purposes of this course, for this is not a course in theology. We have briefly discussed spiritual thinking to enable the student to find a way to contact the hidden **Power** that enables him to solve his problems.

MAN REPRODUCES THE INFINITE NATURE

It has been said that man is created in the image and likeness of God. It would be absurd to think that there is any physical resemblance; therefore, it must be that in his invisible thought-processes man re-enacts the **Infinite** nature, and that in some way he is in the small what God is in the large. This which is true of God must also be true of man. Man's true nature must be a reproduction of God's nature. This is the foundation of the belief in man's right to spiritual healing.

To return to the subject of man's highest thought:

We have said that the higher the thought, the higher the manifestation. Thoughts that are God-like should produce results that are more than human; therefore, when man lets his thoughts rest upon the **Order, Harmony, Wisdom, Power,** and **Love** that characterize the **Infinite,** and when he cultivates these qualities in himself, he will tend to reproduce the **Infinite Creativeness** in his own affairs. It is a **Law** of our thinking that **deeper mind** tends to reproduce in our outer affairs that upon which our **surface mind** most vividly dwells.

TREATMENT — A TURNING TO PERFECTION

Treating for health

We do not "lay on hands" for healing. We do not treat the physical organ. We treat the underlying thought that is causing the illness. The only tool we use is constructive thought, which is more powerful than dynamite.

The wrong way to treat a physical illness would be to center the thought upon the pain and distress and the incurable side of the picture. This would be the way of the world, which prays, "O God, heal my heart, my stomach, my illness."

The Science of Mind way is to turn immediately from all the physical symptoms, and focus the **mind** on our concept of God and of ourselves as reproducing His nature. We turn our thoughts **toward** that which is the very essence of **Order** and **Harmony,** for illness is dis-**Order** and in-**Harmony.** We turn away from the weakness evident in this body, and fill our thoughts with the **Power** that knows no limit, that twirls a planet on its axis and steers it in its course around the sun.

We should put away all thought of the curability or incurability of a condition, and know that we are dealing with a **Power** that is limitless. We should stop thinking of the fact that the doctor has said, "I can do no more," and fill our thoughts with the contemplation of the **Wisdom** that has the exact knowledge of every step of the building process that creates brand-new cells, each stamped with **Wisdom's** own perfection.

In treating ourself or others, we turn away from things of earth, no matter how valid they seem to be, to "heaven"; that is, to our highest possible concept. Illness is never healed by our continued contemplation of it in ourself or others; it is healed by quickly turning our thought to the great unblemished, unsick, un-afraid **Intelligence** within, the **Intelligence** that formed the body in the first place and that certainly knows how to rebuild and restore it.

This does not mean that one should refuse medical assistance in all instances. The accumulated skills and knowledge of the modern physician are highly valuable to society. But while one is receiving material treatment, his thought can be going deeper and higher into the spiritual aspects that are the ultimate **Source** of all healing. As one spiritually minded physician said, "I treat the patient, but God heals him."

In later lessons, I will explain the exact technique of treatment so the student will learn the definite procedure to follow, but at this stage it is necessary first to know the fundamentals that underlie all successful treatment, and we have just had one of them.

Treating for prosperity

In like manner, one would never be able successfully to treat for prosperity if his thought were held steadily on the things he does not have. This suggests stringency. He must learn how to turn, instead, toward that which is forever self sufficient, and which calls upon its own inexhaustible resources whenever anything is needed in manifestation.

The methods of doing this will be brought forth as we proceed further with our lessons.

ELIMINATE NEGATIVE SPEECH

"Set a watch, O Lord, before my mouth; keep the door of my lips," said the Psalmist. This verse embodies another fundamental underlying the giving of successful treatment. We cannot always check our thought, because it is so lightning-fast that it is there before we notice it; but we can school ourselves **never to give utterance to that which is negative.**

Too often we are led into the discussion of the troubles of others. We talk of a neighbor who has lost his job, or whose business has failed, or who has great difficulty making ends meet. In most communities, these are the staples of conversation. We fail to see that we give reality to such conditions in others by taking part in such conversations. In doing this, we give these negative appearances reality in our own belief; and since nothing can happen to us except that in which we believe, we lay the foundation for the same experience in our own lives.

It is not always easy to refrain from such discussion in a group, or with some person who eagerly seizes upon every misfortune of his own or others as a topic of conversation; yet it is vitally necessary that we dissociate ourselves from such a consciousness. The student will have to devise his own method of discouraging such talk without hurting the feelings of his friends, or without being considered unsympathetic. He will soon learn ways to turn the conversation in other directions. If he finds it impossible to shake a person loose from his morbid dwelling on the seamy side of life, he can say as little as possible to him, or else avoid meeting him.

Watch your words

The chief thing for our liberation, however, is that we check our speech whenever we catch ourselves starting such subjects. Students tell us that they never dreamed how much of their conversation was taken up with the morbid experiences of life until they started to "keep the door of their lips."

The world seems to have a hankering for the negative. This can be easily observed by sitting quietly in an ordinary group and listening to the discussion. Much of it centers around "my" operation, So-and-So's drinking, the accident at the corner, the divorce of John and Joan, the children's measles, the cancer drive, and the failure of the boss to appreciate John's excellent work.

The student of the Science of Mind need not be a prig; it is not necessary that he sit tight-lipped and disapproving at the discussion; but he will be cultivating his own spiritual consciousness if he endeavors cheerfully to turn the conversation in a positive, optimistic direction. There are so many happy, hopeful things going on that he will have no difficulty in doing this if he "sets a watch before his mouth."

Handle negative experience in a positive way

"But," someone says, "what if my husband has just lost his job, or we simply cannot afford that television set? Are we to ignore these facts?"

Not at all! But there are positive ways and negative ways of discussing them. Losing a job may be regarded as either an ending or a beginning.

Someone has said that the difference between an optimist and a pessimist is seen in this way: Suppose each has a half glass of water. The pessimist says, "Too bad, my glass is already half empty!" The optimist says, "Good, my glass is still half full!" Same amount of water but two ways of regarding it.

The pessimist says, "I've lost my job. Whatever will I do now?" The optimist says, "Well, that's the end of that. I wonder what bigger opportunity lies before me. I wonder what new road is opening up before me."

We never say, "I can't afford that item." Neither do we deceive ourselves or others about our inability to buy it. We take the constructive, hopeful view by saying, "I think we'll be able to get that television set before long."

In answer to the query, "How's business?" we do not say, "Rotten." We say, "I believe it's picking up."

These are a few very superficial procedures we use in the simpler practice of the Science of Mind.

The student has made considerable progress when he comes to see that no one can ever separate us from our good **but we ourselves.**

Man is never displaced from any desirable situation until he has let his **mental** fingers loosen their hold upon it. He or she may become **mentally** separated from the loved one through carelessness or inattention or 'taking him for granted." He may become separated from his job through complaining of its monotony, or about his fellow workers or about the job in general. He may **mentally** separate himself from his position through fear and anxiety or through the belief that he is not doing good enough work or that he is doing too much work for the pay he receives or through any one of a hundred other mental states. Subconsciously, he **mentally** lets go of his job or his mate without ever dreaming that this is what is happening.

It is an action entirely in his **deeper mind.** This paves the way for the physical separation from the job or the person.

The positive way of regarding the losing of a job is this:

I am always in my right place. I am always at the place where I belong by right of my consciousness.

If I have become separated from the job through my negative approach, I start right now to learn. I begin now to alter my inner consciousness so that I am steadily **united** with my good.

If I have outgrown this opportunity, I know that another and better job is now awaiting me, one for which I am better qualified.

I resolutely put behind me any complaint or resentment, for this is a new beginning, in which life moves onto a higher level.

Then, with a watch set upon his lips, he studiously avoids expressing rancor, bitterness, or discouragement. To friends who would commiserate with him, he turns a deaf ear, refusing to listen to their, "It's a dirty shame, John!"

Why does he do this? Wouldn't it be more honest to say, "Yes, I got a raw deal," because that was what happened? The answer is no, because it would only tend to perpetuate the state of mind that led to his dismissal. If he sees **why** and **how** we attract experiences, he will honestly know that we unconsciously attract our own "raw deals."

There are two ways of reacting to misfortune. The negative is, "Why should this happen to **me**?" The positive is, "**What** has this to teach me?" or "What **good** can it yield me?" or "**What** in me brought this upon me?"

EVERY EFFECT HAS AN ADEQUATE CAUSE

The student who has absorbed the teaching so far knows that whether he can trace it or not, it must have been some loosening of his **mental** fingers that led to his separation from his good. Nothing in his life ever comes by chance; everything comes by the **Law of Cause and Effect.** Nothing ever just "happens" to us. For every **effect**, there is always an adequate and consistent **cause.**

We deny this **Law** when we complain about what life hands us, and thus we place ourselves in the position where our next step may lead to our becoming a discouraged whiner and complainer. If we allow this to go on, we can develop a fully matured persecution complex, which can mean the end of all constructive thinking and consequently of all advancement.

We offset this gloomy ultimate by bringing in our valuable words, "I **choose.**" Regardless of the discouraged way we feel, we say:

I **choose** to believe I am well regarded and well received by every person I meet. My talents and abilities are known and recognized by those I meet. My efforts are well rewarded. My activities are fruitful. Mentally I take my place among those who get what they go after.

At first, we might find something within ourselves denying the truth we utter. This traitorous voice within us might continue to whisper, "You know you are failing. You have always failed. Stop kidding yourself and face your own inadequacy."

This is the critical point. We must quietly and firmly decide to **choose** the kind of thought that we drop as seed into the garden of our **deeper mind** just as we would deliberately **choose** to plant a specially selected peach seedling even though we had never grown a peach tree before.

We maintain the quiet assurance that this thought we are planting will grow just as surely as the peach seedling will grow when planted in the suitable environment of the earth.

Look within for causes

The untutored or unscientific thinker always looks **outside** himself for the cause of his miseries. The person who is spiritually scientific always looks **within** for the basic reason. Even when he seems unable to locate the origin of his trouble, he sticks to the fact that his **outer** world of affairs is only his **inner** world of consciousness brought down into form.

This checks his complaint at the outset. It makes of every unhappy condition not an ending but a beginning. It keeps him with a constructive view of life, and continually turns him away from the morbid. It keeps him from hating anyone, because even though some other person's actions seem unfair, he knows that something **within** himself must have drawn forth those actions, and he determines to weed the garden of his thought so that it will not occur again.

NEW MENTAL HABITS CAN BE FORMED

The place where his progress starts is at his lips where he checks the expression of his negative thoughts. As he practices this, he will soon notice that this sort of thought comes less and less frequently, often within seven days. Ultimately his new tendency of mind will become the starting point of his progress.

It is somewhat like the situation of the farmer driving home from market. His horse had become so habituated to turning in at the farm entrance that when he bought a farm a mile beyond the original one, he had to tug on the reins to keep the horse from turning in as he passed the old entrance. He had to repeat this firmly on many occasions until the horse became habituated to the idea that the old entrance was not his any more. Eventually, he went by of his own accord.

Deeper mind can be taught a habit just as a horse can be. It requires the steady practice of "I **choose**" regardless of what **deeper mind** has been habituated to feel. We can change the states of **deeper mind**.

But until this happens, we can make a good start at the point where our thoughts form into words, at our lips; and we must **practice** it. One knows that he could not become a facile violin player without daily practice. Just as assiduous practice of the techniques will make an accomplished violinist, so will daily practice of spiritual techniques lead to happy, healthy, successful living.

Here is an important fundamental in the practice of the Science of Mind:

Never say a thing about yourself that you do not want to see realized in your life.

SPECIAL HELPS IN STUDY AND PRACTICAL APPLICATION

These special helps have been carefully prepared to help you get the most out of this course.

Questions on the lesson

I advise that you first study the lesson carefully, then put it aside, write the answers to the questions, and, finally, **check your answers by the lesson.**

Keep the answers as a running commentary on the course **for your own benefit.** At its conclusion, you will find they have become a record of your own growth in consciousness.

1. Why does our thought have power?

2. What is the underlying difference between materialistic and spiritual thinking?

3. What does our outer world (state of health, finances, personal relationships, etc.) reveal about the state of our thought-life?

4. What is the highest thought of which man is capable?

5. What does an objective view of the universe tell us about God?

6. What does being created in the image and likeness of God mean?

7. What is the first fundamental in successful treatment?

8. Why is the eliminating of negative speech emphasized in this lesson?

9. What is the positive way of handling negative experiences?

10. What must always precede the outer experience?

Collateral reading suggestions

Please keep in mind my comments on the suggestions as I gave them for Lesson I.

Frederick Bailes:　　Hidden Power for Human Problems, Chs. 2 and 3

"Is There a Cure for Frustration?"

Your Mind Can Heal You, Ch. I (1971), Ch. II (1941)

Claude Bristol:　　The Magic of Believing

Practical application

. . . thought-training

As a starting point to eliminate negative thought, eliminate negative speech.

"Set a watch before my mouth; keep the door of my lips."

A simple test for positive speech is this:

Do I want this thing that I am saying about myself (or about another) realized in my life?

. . . writing suggestion

Set down the five attributes of God as given in this lesson, add others from your own observation, experience, or other source of knowledge, and list under each as many evidences of it as you can.

You will find it helpful to keep this in a convenient place in your notebook, and add to it throughout the course.

. . . a treatment for general good

My **mind** is an inlet of the **Infinite Ocean of Mind.**

In its depth lies all knowledge of past, present, and future.

In it are deep levels untouched by any surface influences.

In it lies the healing **Power** of the **Infinite Wisdom,** that "Light which lighteth every man who cometh into the world."

In it lie the answer to every problem, freedom from every fetter, healing for every condition, balm for every hurt.

My **mind,** as an inlet of the **Infinite Ocean of Mind,** has **power** to renew itself, to alter its patterns, to rise into the place of dominance over illness, lack, and inharmony.

My **mind** is God's **Mind** in me this day.

And it **is** so.

Lesson 3

THE FOCUS
OF ATTENTION

MENTAL ATTITUDES

Never belittle yourself
Act out the part of the person you want to be
Turn away from past failures
Turn to past successes no matter how small

LIFE PAYS US WHAT WE ASK

POWER FLOWS TO THE FOCUS OF ATTENTION

THE LAW OF ATTRACTION

MAN'S MIND IS OF THE ONE MIND

There is a **Knower** within us
Infinite Creativeness invests man's thought
— the dominant pattern emerges

MENTAL ATTITUDES, continued

THE SCIENCE OF MIND IS A WAY OF LIFE

HABITS — A MATTER OF CONSCIOUSNESS

THIRD LESSON
GOALS

To understand:

> What is meant by "the focus of attention"
> Why **Power Flows to the Focus of Attention**
> How the **Law of Attraction** operates in our lives

To make a definite beginning in cultivating the
basic mental attitudes

MENTAL ATTITUDES

As previously indicated, the early lessons of this course deal with the basic mental attitudes underlying the specific methods of treating definitely for specific results. In this lesson, I shall emphasize and expand upon this fundamental statement in Lesson 2.

Never say a thing about yourself that you do not want to see realized in your life.

Never belittle yourself

In speaking of setting a watch upon our lips, we refer now to a very common practice, that of belittling ourself, our talents and abilities, our achievements. It is a minimizing of our strong points and a ballooning of our weak points. A little of this may be due to modesty; but the larger proportion actually grows out of a general sense of inferiority, and is done for the purpose of having someone else bolster our morale. The person who does this is not sure of himself. He craves reassurance and seeks this way of finding it or having it handed to him.

It is not easy to plunge to the center of the problem and immediately build an awareness of our own worth, but we can approach it by practicing a procedure that would be quite natural for us if we already had the inner consciousness of our true worth.

Act out the part of the person you want to be

We can **decide** what sort of person we would like to be and begin at once to act the part. One who does this usually finds that he comes to think within himself as he wants to think. We are, however, under **no** circumstances, to act the part with the intention of impressing others. What others think of us at this stage is not important; and while we might succeed in fooling them, we could never fool ourselves. It is ourselves only that we are dealing with now, and we must deal honestly. What we think of ourselves is the chief thing.

If, as sometimes happens, we should have a return of that feeling that we're "not so much," we must instantly make up our minds that we will never again voice it. This will stop the drift toward the negative.

We must never forget that the power of the spoken word is far greater than we imagine. Even though he does not fully believe the truth of what he says, the person who insists, "I have no personality," or "I am not attractive," is giving himself a treatment from the negative side, which will tend to make him unattractive.

33

To say, "I am never able to hold a job," will set a current of energy in motion that will continue to result in his losing jobs. "I always get the bad breaks," or "I always do the wrong thing at the right time," are expressions that gain terrific force once they are put into words, especially if they are repeated from time to time.

There is a reason for this. Today is the finished product of yesterday's or last year's thought. Today's thought, even now passing through the **loom of mind,** will become the pattern of to-morrow's or next year's experience. That which we now are think-ing will take form, sometime, somewhere.

If we hope to get free from those negative, unwanted condi-tions we have been voicing, we must change our thought. And if we have not yet advanced to the point where we have thorough control over our thoughts, we can, at least to a large degree, con-trol our speech; therefore, **today** we refuse to give utterance to that which we now know will only perpetuate our unwanted past experiences.

Turn away from past failures

The person who reaches backward to stress the points at which he made mistakes or a wrong choice, or failed to impress others, thereby places those negative things in the forefront of his consciousness, and his **loom of mind** has no choice but to weave them into similar experiences tomorrow. It is done unto us as we believe; and if we believe that we made blunders yes-terday, then it follows that we shall make blunders tomorrow, for we are expressing our belief in blunders. If we believe people were not attracted to us yesterday, then we believe they will not be attracted tomorrow. And so it is with every negative belief.

This is why the student, from now on, should speak only of those things he wants to see realized in his life.

Turn to past successes no matter how small

Having assumed a positive attitude, we can now recall the times when we made the right **decisions,** or when someone showed a decided liking for our company, or when we made the right **choice** or got the "good breaks." We may think of the times when we showed to good advantage when competing with others. We may recall sincere compliments paid us. And, being very care-ful not to become a boastful bore, we may even speak of our achievements, for we are now trying hard to reverse our previous negative underlying trend of thought, and anything that feeds our belief in our true worth is grist for our mill.

We call to mind any compliment ever given us, even those we felt were insincere, for, although the insincere person thought he was "putting one over" on us, we turn it inside out and read our own meaning into it, knowing that any action, any utterance, becomes to us that which we want to make it.

Now the student may make a quiet **decision:**

I will never say a thing about myself that I do not want to see realized in my life.

This one **decision** has changed the lives of thousands.

LIFE PAYS US WHAT WE ASK

Life is never unfair to us. We are unfair to ourselves. Ours is the **choice:** we may offer ourselves in the bargain basement or in the exclusive section, and **Life** is not only willing to pay; it has no alternative but to pay the exact price we set upon ourselves. It can pay no more, no less, because it is as impartial as the mirror, which must reflect exactly what is placed before it. It is as impersonal as the loom, which must weave into cloth the threads that are given it, be they cheap white cotton or costly threads of silk.

"My Wage," by Jessie B. Rittenhouse, says this very well:

I bargained with Life for a penny,
And Life would pay no more,
However I begged at evening
When I counted my scanty store;

For Life is a just employer;
He gives you what you ask,
But once you have set the wages,
Why, you must bear the task.

I worked for a menial's hire,
Only to learn, dismayed,
That any wage I had asked of Life
Life would have paid. *

When we come to see this, **Life** no longer will seem harsh and cruel to us. Our world will change as our ideas concerning ourselves change. So never be afraid to think highly of your value.

This implies making ourselves valuable. The shirker, constantly watching the clock or giving inadequate service, should not expect to lie on his back, filling his thought with the picture of his worth, and imagining that **Infinite Mind** will bring this latter picture into form.

*Quoted from Jessie B. Rittenhouse's **Door of Dreams,** with the permission of Houghton Mifflin Company, Boston.

35

One may fool his employer; he can never fool the **Law.** He is avoiding his rightful responsibilities; therefore, **Mind** will give him what he most deeply wants — a life devoid of responsibility. But it will also be devoid of rewards. Since **Life's** biggest rewards are coupled with biggest responsibilities, in avoiding responsibility he is avoiding reward.

POWER FLOWS TO THE FOCUS OF ATTENTION

It might be well at this point to consider the difficulty of constantly maintaining positive attitudes. As human beings, subject to the limitations of our common humanity, we find that, in spite of our earnest desire to maintain the highest level of thinking, negative thoughts continue to creep up on us. When the untutored find the old pattern showing up from time to time, they are likely to abandon their efforts in disgust. In the Science of Mind, however, we know that this is neither disastrous nor final, for: **Power Flows to the Focus of Attention.**

To help the student understand what we mean by "the focus of attention," we shall begin with a concrete example taken from our outer world. The student himself may illustrate this by standing at his front door and looking steadily at — let us say — an outstanding house-number directly across the street. He will see that number distinctly because he is focusing his attention on it; but as he looks at it, without moving his eyes, he will also be conscious of things on either side. These become increasingly vague as they are more to the right or to the left of the house-number, which is the focal point of his attention.

We shall now move to the world of thought. The Focus of Attention chart represents man's consciousness from one point of view. Man has central consciousness, and he has marginal consciousness, just as he has central vision and marginal vision. In his central consciousness are those things of which he is most vividly aware and which obtrude themselves upon his thought most often or most forcefully. In his marginal consciousness are those things of which he is only dimly aware.

THE FOCUS OF ATTENTION

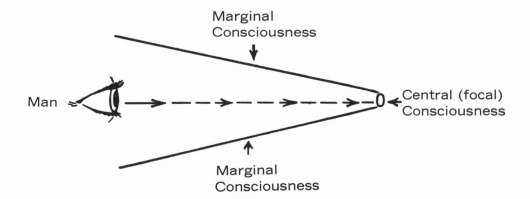

Man's **mind** is like a funnel.

Power Flows to the Focus of Attention

If we belittle ourselves, **Power** flowing through that thought about ourselves will manifest it in our experience.

If we build an awareness of our own true worth, **Power** flowing through that thought about ourselves will manifest it in our experience.

If we keep our past failures at the center of our attention, **Power** flowing through that thought will keep failure in our life.

If we turn to past successes no matter how small, **Power** flowing through that thought will bring more success into our life.

If we let hostility — with its grudges, resentments, and criticism — take the focus of our attention, we are thrown out of tune with the **Creative Flow.**

If we cultivate a sincere well-wishing for the good of others, we bring ourselves into tune with the **Creative Flow.**

Power Flows to the Focus of Attention

THE LAW OF ATTRACTION

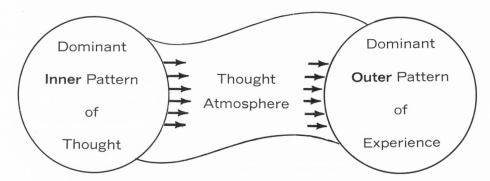

The **Law of Attraction** is that activity of **Mind** that draws to us that which is like our Dominant **Inner** Pattern of Thought.

Our Dominant **Inner** Pattern of Thought determines
our Thought Atmosphere,
and
Our Thought Atmosphere determines
our Dominant **Outer** Pattern of Experience.

We all carry our own Thought Atmosphere, which is the image of our thought, and which people tend to sense no matter what we say.

Our Thought Atmosphere determines their response to us.

Our Dominant **Inner** Pattern of Thought becomes our Dominant **Outer** Pattern of Experience.

We attract what we love, hate, fear, expect, or steadily contemplate.

Our **outer** world is our **inner** world objectified.

I suppose no man can violate his nature. . . . We pass for what we are. . . . Men imagine that they communicate their virtue or vice only by overt actions, and do not see that virtue or vice emit a breath every moment.

Don't **say** things. What you are stands over you the while, and thunders so that I cannot hear what you say to the contrary. — Emerson

By **selecting** new "spools" of thought, we can change our Dominant **Inner** Pattern of Thought and thus our Thought Atmosphere and our Dominant **Outer** Pattern of Experience.

The Law of Attraction Is as Scrupulously Fair as a Mirror.

THE LAW OF ATTRACTION

Man tends to attract that which he loves, fears, or steadily expects; that is, those things that he keeps at his central (focal) consciousness.

Man fears certain negative experiences, and, quite logically, he attracts them. But the student has made up his mind that from now on, he is definitely going to love his most cherished desire above everything else; therefore, as often as possible, he is going to draw it into the focus of his attention. There will come times when the negative will edge toward the center, but the instant he notices this, he will immediately say "I resist that suggestion" and he will again bring back into focus that good that he wishes, and surround it with his love. Gradually, he will notice that the good, more and more, tends to stay at the center, while the negative tends to fade away.

MAN'S MIND IS OF THE ONE MIND

There is a good reason why **Power Flows to the Focus of Attention.** The **mind** of man is not something separate; it is part of the **One Intelligence,** which formed and sustains the universe. Man's brain structure is the best on earth, far surpassing that of the highest animal; yet it has certain limitations. While man's **mind** is historical, in that it can look backward and recall the past, it is not strongly prophetic; that is, it cannot look forward and with any certainty foretell the future. Though it has other limitations, we mention this one just as an illustration.

Limited as man's **mind** is, however, it is still a part of the **Infinite Intelligence** and is forever united with it. This **Infinite Intelligence,** carrying all ideas in their perfection, is like an ageless river ever flowing through the brain of man.

There is a Knower within us

All man's future inventions and discoveries are at this moment in that **river.** As it flows through the brains of men whose habitual thought tends toward some particular idea and concept, those men catch and register new ideas in line with their concepts. That is why men on opposite sides of the earth who have never known each other sometimes come forth simultaneously with the same invention, the same discovery, the same story theme. Each one believes that he, personally, originated the idea; but no human being ever really originates. He merely — to change the anology — tunes in on ideas carried in the **One Great Originating Mind.**

Infinite Creativeness invests man's thought

Earlier we said that man is in the small what God is in the large. **Creativeness** is of God. Man's thought is creative because

God's thought flows through it, as electrical current flows through a microphone "boosting" the voice far beyond its normal power. The thoughts of a person are small and weak in comparison with those of the **Infinite;** but being of the same nature as that of the **Infinite,** they are "boosted" to something far beyond the human. When the Great Teacher said, "The Father in me, He it is that doeth the works," he was pointing the way for anyone to have power.

If we imagine our chart illustrating the focus of attention as a funnel through which all the **Power** and **Creativeness** of the **Infinite** flows, then we can see that when a man draws a particular idea to the center of his thought, it is flowed through by that central stream of the **Infinite Power.** Those thoughts that are along the margins of consciousness are not subjected to this **Creative Flow** to the same degree. It follows, therefore, that the fleeting, dimly conceived thought has less power than that which is steadily held toward the center. We can make this even more emphatic: **That which lies at the focus of man's attention is bound to come forth.**

— the dominant pattern emerges

This does not mean that one idea must be held to the exclusion of all others, nor does it mean that our desired manifestation will not come forth if our thinking is a mixture of positive and negative. Since man is far from perfect, the thinking of the best and most successful persons is mixed; but it has been proved that, despite varied thinking, if one's dominant desire is held more or less steadily at the center of his attention and affection, it will manifest. "Let us not be weary in welldoing, for in due season we shall reap if we faint not."

MENTAL ATTITUDES, continued

Another basic attitude that makes for success in demonstration is that of love. This word has been thrown about so lightly, even loosely, and has been surrounded by such an atmosphere of "stickiness" that I hesitate to use it. It might be better to say that all hostility must be removed from the heart if one would make demonstrations. Since we have seen that **Harmony** is basic in the universe, it follows that hostility throws us out of tune with the **Creative Flow.** "Love is the fulfilling of the **Law.**" Hostility is the obstructing of the **Law.**

It is apparent that hatred and love cannot occupy the same place at the same moment. It should, therefore, be apparent that man cannot demonstrate his own good while wishing that someone else be kept from his good. Grudges, resentment, and criticism can effectually stop our demonstration, because, as a rule, they are so intense that they automatically rush to the focus of attention.

To understand all would be to forgive all. If we could know all the influences that have played upon the person who has wronged us, we might understand why he has acted as he has. If those same influences had assailed us with equal force, we might have done just as he did. At any rate, harboring a grudge or resentment will block our achievement of good. It is too high a price to pay. The person against whom hostility is held is not hurt by it; it is the person who harbors it who is the loser. The practice of the spirit of understanding will make us gentle. It is one of the most enriching attitudes one can cultivate.

THE SCIENCE OF MIND IS A WAY OF LIFE

It can be seen that the Science of Mind involves one's whole way of life. It is impossible to cultivate love for mankind in general and at the same time retain a tiny corner of our thought for feelings of hostility toward an individual; for if, with all our good hanging in the balance, our hostility is still important enough or appealing enough for us to hang on to, it will also have an appeal powerful enough to color all the rest of our thinking, and effectually block our treatment for others and our own pathway into the land of our heart's desire.

All that a person is goes into his treatment. Not alone the words of his mouth must be acceptable, but also the meditation of his heart.

Some students want to be rid of their illnesses, their poverty, or some other handicap; yet at the same time they cling to their meannesses or their pet neuroses. This cannot be done. "Except a man be born again, he cannot see the kingdom of God." He not only cannot enter it; he cannot even see it. "Old things are passed away; all things are become new." He is born into a new way of life, a new way of thinking. Where this is done thoroughly, his eyes look out upon a different world. He is born again. He has become a new man.

There must be, for the student, a rightabout-face, an altering of his whole life; for he is now shifting his thought from the world's way to God's way; from the human, material way to the spiritual way. There must be sincerity of purpose when he takes the pathway to the fulfillment of his deepest desires, a clearing out of the old and a bringing in of the new. "Men do not put new wine into old bottles . . . but they put new wine into new bottles."

The Science of Mind is not simply something added to our belief in order to make us well and prosperous. It demands all of the student. If he gives it, it will flood his life with the Good. The student who practices it sincerely and intelligently should begin to see very definite results within seven days.

HABITS — A MATTER OF CONSCIOUSNESS

Students sometimes wonder whether they must give up certain habits in order to make their demonstration. We are not keepers of morals and, at this point, place no restrictions upon the student. We feel that each person can and will make his own decisions about his habits. The student probably will continue with whatever he is doing until he has a persistent uneasy feeling about it. Then, whatever he quits, or whatever new habit he takes on, will be as a result of his own growing **consciousness,** and will therefore be right for him.

Standards of morals and ethics vary so much that no teacher can tell anyone what is "good" or "bad." To some, the eating of flesh is bad; to others, the use of tea, coffee, tobacco, or alcohol is reprehensible. Habits that are accepted in some countries are frowned upon in others. It is not so long ago that a person would be refused membership in some churches unless he promised to forsake theater, cards, dancing. Today they are a part of church activities. "There is nothing either good or bad but thinking makes it so." Quite obviously, this does not refer to gross sins but only to those debatable and minor details of one's personal life.

Each one must decide for himself. The guide should be, "Does this practice hinder my spiritual development, or is it definitely destructive to me or to someone else?" If so, it should be out of the life.

SPECIAL HELPS IN STUDY
AND PRACTICAL APPLICATION

These special helps have been carefully prepared to help you get the most out of this course.

Questions on the lesson

I advise that you first study the lesson carefully, then put it aside, write the answers to the questions, and, finally, **check your answers by the lesson.**

Keep the answers as a running commentary on the course **for your own benefit.** At its conclusion, you will find they have become a record of your own growth in consciousness.

1. What is a beginning step that we can take in building a consciousness of our true worth?

2. Why is it of such importance that we build this consciousness?

3. How should we regard the past?

4. Explain **Power Flows to the Focus of Attention.**

5. How does that relate to the **Law of Attraction?**

6. Why is that which lies at the focus of man's attention bound to come forth?

7. Why is an attitude of love an absolute essential in the making of demonstrations?

8. What attitude must we take toward those who act wrongly?

9. Comment on "The Science of Mind involves the whole life."

10. What determines one's habits?

Collateral reading suggestions

Please recall again my comments on these suggestions as I gave them in Lesson I.

Frederick Bailes: "Getting What You Go After"

Hidden Power for Human Problems, Ch. 5

Ernest Holmes: This Thing Called Life

Practical application

. . . thought-training

Continue in line with last lesson, using the basic mental attitudes as your guide:

I will not say a thing about myself that I do not want realized in my life.

. . . writing suggestion

Make a list of those desired conditions that you are going to keep in the focus of your attention.

. . . a treatment for general good

This day I increase my awareness of the **River of Mind** flowing through me.

I am healed of the distortion that saw only the debris on the surface.

My clearer vision now sees through to the **Reality** beneath, to the pure, untainted streaming of the **Infinite,** and my healing is completed as I come alive to the **River** as it is alive to me.

The **River of Perfect Mind** manifests this day in me as life.

It now overflows my consciousness as joy.

It now bathes my entire being as peace.

It now fills my every need and turns into a Niagara of abundance.

It is a river of physical healing to me and mine.

My good is so great that it spills over into the lives of others and sets their good in motion.

Thus I become a blessing to all who come into contact with me this day.

And it **is** so.

Lesson 4

WHY MAN'S MIND IS CREATIVE

THE ONE CREATIVE PROCESS

THREEFOLD NATURE OF THE INFINITE

HOW THE CREATIVE CYCLE OPERATES (Charts)
Spirit selects and initiates
Mind obeys
Body, Unformed Substance, is molded into form

God is all — and in all

MAN ALSO IS A trinity OF spirit, mind, AND body
Surface mind selects and initiates
Deeper mind obeys
Body reflects man's thought

SPIRIT IS CAUSE — MIND IS CREATIVE MEDIUM
Genesis describes the **Creative Process**

SPIRIT HAS THE POWERS OF SELECTION AND INITIATIVE
Progress comes from using selection and initiative

MAN'S CONCEPT OF GOD IS GROWING
What is God's will?

WHY ILLNESS DEVELOPS IN MAN

Surface mind MUST SELECT POSITIVE THOUGHTS
Reason and choice must control the feelings
On waking up ''blue''
Deeper mind can be re-educated

FOURTH LESSON
GOALS

To come into a clearer understanding
of why man's **mind** is creative

To make definite use of the powers
of **selection** and **initiative**

Lessons 1, 2, and 3 have been devoted chiefly to two matters: (1) an understanding of the power of thought, with something of the reason why, and (2) specific suggestions as to how to improve the quality of one's thought.

The student who has come into this understanding and is following the suggestions is finding that as his thought improves in quality, his circumstances improve correspondingly.

But the earnest and inquiring student will want to know more of the "why." Moreover, he will find that as he does know more of the "why," his power to bring about definite, specific results will increase.

In this lesson the student is brought into a deeper and more metaphysical aspect of the Science of Mind. I urge you to study it carefully, going over it several times. Come back to it again and again. It will enable you to make very sure that you have a clear understanding of the difference between the activity of **surface mind** (selecting and initiating), as characterized by "I choose," and that of **deeper mind** (fabricating), as characterized by "I **obey**" (obedience). Success in getting what you want from life depends on understanding these different activities.

When you have clearly grasped that, you will have a sense of authority when you "speak your word," or "treat." You will no longer wonder whether results will follow; you will know they will, because you will have within yourself the deep conviction of the **Power** and **Reality** of the thing you are working with. Once you have mastered this phase of it, the remainder of the course will fall naturally into place.

It is natural that man should want to draw into his experience those desirable things that are not there now. Thus every "demonstration" is an act of creation. That which man desires must be created. When we find the **general Principle** of creation, we can apply it to the **particular.** There is such a **Principle,** of course, traceable throughout the universe. It is the selfsame **Principle** and method through which our world came into being.

THE ONE CREATIVE PROCESS

In **The Creative Process in the Individual,** Judge Thomas Troward has done a masterly work of delineating this **Principle.** I recommend that you add this book to your library, and study it carefully. Some may find it a little difficult to read, but return to it again and again, for it will amply repay the time and effort given to it.

(Incidentally, it was the reading and deep study of this book that led to my healing of diabetes more than fifty years ago.)

Troward was a devout Episcopalian. As a judge in India, he also studied deeply the religions and philosophies of the country, and found certain similarities in the philosophies underlying the religions of East and West.

He wrote the book early in this century before many of our scientific discoveries were made. Though some of the scientific terms he uses are now outmoded, the principle as he advanced it stands stronger today than when he advanced it. It is a metaphysical principle in line with modern science. The student who masters Troward has a solid rock of metaphysical healing philosophy under his feet.

Troward's thesis is that there is only one **Creative Process** in the universe. It brought the world at large into being; every moment it is bringing man's personal world into being. By this process, a star is created, or a body healed. And if we would bring into our lives something good that is not there now, we shall be able to do it only if we use the same **Creative Process** and method that the **Originating Intelligence** used.

In order to grasp this, the student will start with an inquiry into the nature of God, or, to use Troward's term, the **Originating Intelligence.**

Troward starts with the well-known fact that matter — even though it is hard and solid and has weight — is only energy, or force, in form. It is quite evident that in the beginning there was no universe in solid form; yet all the material out of which the universe would be formed was present in an unformed state, as the unformed "**Body** of God." In the beginning, there was only God — and **nothing,** since at that time there was no material universe.

The energy that caused the universe to be formed could only have been an energy that does not originate in the material sphere. The only known form of energy that does not arise out of matter is — **thought.** But there were no people in existence; so the thought must have been that of an **Infinite Thinker.** The eminent physicist Sir James Jeans, in a purely scientific way, arrives at this same conclusion as we shall show in our next lesson.

THREEFOLD NATURE OF THE INFINITE

The three-sided nature of **Infinite Intelligence** is somewhat difficult to comprehend. Perhaps a simple illustration will make it clear.

Think of a block of ice. We know it is ice and nothing else; yet it is water, and with a slight change can become steam.

Placed in a pail on a hot stove, the ice soon becomes water, which is ice at a higher molecular vibration. Its molecules are moving at a higher rate than when it was ice.

Apply more heat, and the water now becomes steam, a still higher vibration. Thus there have been three different substances, each with a different name; yet they are all basically one, differing only in their vibratory rate.

Each functions differently from the other. As steam, this substance will clean the grease off an automobile motor, which ice or water will not do. Ice will keep fruit fresh, which steam will not do. Water will serve as the abode of fish, which neither steam nor ice will do.

Thus we have a diversity of name, form, and function for the same thing; yet under whatever name and whatever function it acts, its basic, essential chemical character is the same, namely H_2O.

Suppose we reverse the procedure. Invisible steam emerging from the kettle spout becomes visible vapor; passed over or through a cool coil, it becomes water; refrigerated, it becomes ice. Each gradation becomes more dense or "solid" than the preceding one.

Now suppose we think of **Spirit** as the highest vibration in the **Trinity,** invisible like the steam in its activity. It **selects** what is to be done, and **initiates** the **Creative Cycle.** Its decisions are not seen by us until **Mind,** a lower vibration, manifests them by acting upon the **Primary Unformed Substance** to condense it into form **(Body),** a still lower vibration. At this point, the **Creative Sequence** has been completed.

I regret having to use such a crude analogy, but the Unseen must sometimes be depicted in terms of the seen, the Unknown in terms of the known, since all of us are still in that kindergarten stage of development where we must use the physical senses to interpret spiritual truth.

HOW THE CREATIVE CYCLE OPERATES

In **The Creative Process in the Individual,** Troward's keen legal mind presents a most logical case showing how the **Three-in-One** operates.

Let us see, then, how creation evidently occurs, remembering that as God the greater **Trinity** creates a universe, man the smaller **trinity** creates any good that he desires.

Spirit, Mind, and **Unformed Substance** are one and have always been present. Scientists tell us that matter must always have been present in an unformed state. No one of the **Three** has created the others. (Troward speaks of **Spirit containing** the **Primary Substance,** and then **projecting,** or **evolving,** not creating, it.)

There is an equality among these three phases of the **Trinity** since they have all been present throughout the eternity that is past, but, for some inscrutable reason, there is a division of function. Perhaps it is only the way we **see** its operation, there being no real division, but only an apparent division of function.

We may use an imperfect analogy, and call **Spirit** the Architect. As part of its indivisible Being, it has **Mind** the Builder, and **Unformed Substance,** the Building Materials.

An architect **(Spirit)** brings his plans to the master builder and says, "Follow these out." The builder **(Mind),** without the slightest sense of inferiority, takes them and complies with the directions. He knows that the architect specializes in the drawing of plans but not in building. He, the builder, does not draw plans but specializes in building. It is by the co-operation of these two that all the beautiful and massive structures in the world are erected out of unformed materials such as wood, rock, etc.

So God as **Spirit** and God as **Mind,** two phases of the **One,** acting separately, are working in closest harmony. Neither is inferior to the other; they act as equal partners.

In like manner, there is no division between man's **surface mind** and his **deeper mind.** They work together. The **surface mind selects** and presents the blueprint, while **deeper mind fabricates** it into form, two phases of one activity.

Charts

The CREATIVE PROCESS

in the UNIVERSE and in the INDIVIDUAL

The charts on the **Creative Process** in the universe and in the individual require careful and diligent study. Each idea is of the utmost importance.

Those students who grasp their meaning and implications invariably produce effects far in advance of those who fail to do so.

The more you study them, the more clearly you will see the **obedient** response of this vast **Creative Power** to your conscious **choices.**

It removes treatment from a vague, hit-or-miss dependence upon "wishing" or "feeling" to an authoritative **knowing,** such as the **Infinite** has.

Refer to them constantly as you study this lesson.

The CREATIVE PROCESS in the UNIVERSE and in the INDIVIDUAL

The three phases of the **Infinite Intelligence,** acting as one, complete the one **Creative Process.**

By this process, it is thought God brought the universe into being.

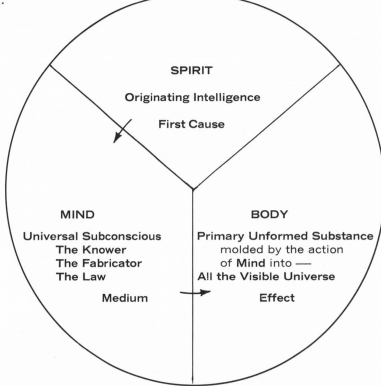

By **this same process,** man brings his world of experience into being.

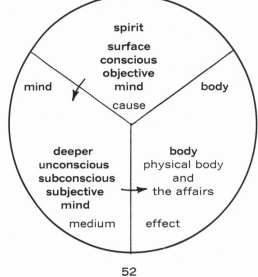

The CREATIVE PROCESS in the UNIVERSE and in the INDIVIDUAL

WHAT GOD IS IN THE LARGE . . . man is in the small
"the image and likeness of God"

SPIRIT — First Cause

1. **Selection**
   Selects a desired form and
   thinks of itself as
   expressing it

2. **Initiative:** "Let there be."
   Initiates the action of
   Mind and starts it
   fabricating the form
   Always acts on **Mind**
   Never acted on by anything

MIND — Medium

1. **Obedience** to **Spirit**
   Always acted on by **Spirit**
   Always acts on **Body**

2. **Fabrication** into form of
   Spirit's choices

surface mind (spirit) — cause

1. **Selection**
   "I choose."
   We watch the "spools"
   we put on the "loom."

2. **Initiative**
   "I direct the **Creative Process**
   toward a given end."
   We start a course of action.
   Always acts on **deeper mind**
   Need never be acted on
   by anything

deeper mind (mind) — medium

1. **Obedience** to **surface mind**
   Always acted on by **surface mind**
   Always acts on **body**

2. **Fabrication** into form of
   surface mind's choices

Omniscience — **Wisdom of the Ages** — **The Knower**
   Omniscience will never be faced with a problem too great.
   Omniscience knows how to build a star or a cell, a great corporation
   or a peanut stand.

Omnipotence — **All-Power** — **the Doer**
   The biggest thing to us is infinitesimal to **Omnipotence**.
   To **Omnipotence**, there is no "big" or "little," "hard" or "easy,"
   "simple" or "complex," "curable" or "incurable."

Omnipresence — **Everywhere-present**
   Mind presses in on us as definitely as does the atmosphere.
   "Closer is He than breathing, and nearer than hands and feet."
   — Tennyson

   "I only know I cannot drift beyond His love and care." — Whittier

   "St. Augustine described the nature of God as a circle whose center
   is everywhere and its circumference nowhere." — Emerson

BODY — **Effect**

Inertia
Always acted on by **Mind**
Never acts on anything

body — effect

Inertia
Always acted on by **deeper mind**
Never acts on anything
   Never inflicts anything on us
   No power to originate
   or heal a condition

The CREATIVE PROCESS in the UNIVERSE

The three phases of the **Infinite Intelligence,** acting as one, complete the one **Creative Process.**

By this process, it is thought God brought the universe into being.

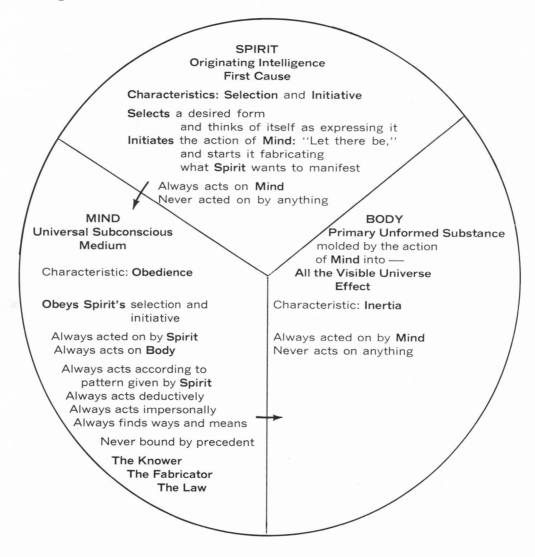

THE THREEFOLD NATURE OF GOD THE iNFINITE..........

THE MACROCOSM ....

WHAT GOD THE INFINITE IS IN THE LARGE....................

The CREATIVE PROCESS in the INDIVIDUAL

By **this same process,** man brings his world of experience into being.

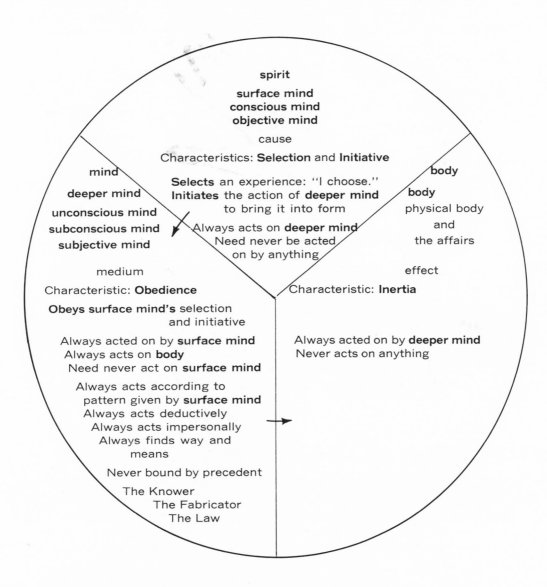

spirit

surface mind
conscious mind
objective mind

cause

Characteristics: **Selection** and **Initiative**

mind

deeper mind

unconscious mind

subconscious mind

subjective mind

Selects an experience: "I choose."
Initiates the action of **deeper mind**
to bring it into form
Always acts on **deeper mind**
Need never be acted
on by anything

body

body

physical body
and
the affairs

effect

medium

Characteristic: **Obedience**

Obeys surface mind's selection
and initiative

Always acted on by **surface mind**
Always acts on **body**
Need never act on **surface mind**

Always acts according to
pattern given by **surface mind**
Always acts deductively
Always acts impersonally
Always finds way and
means

Never bound by precedent

The Knower
The Fabricator
The Law

Characteristic: **Inertia**

Always acted on by **deeper mind**
Never acts on anything

.... the threefold nature of man the finite

.... the microcosm

.... man the finite is in the small — "the image and likeness of God"

(As I said at the beginning of this lesson, the more you know of the "why," the more you will be able to bring about specific results. The more you master the underlying **Principles** that are operating beneath the surface when you are giving a treatment, the more certainty you have in the outcome of your treatment because you know it is based upon principle, the **Law of Mind.**)

Spirit selects and initiates

Troward shows how there evidently was in the **Originating Intelligence** the desire for creation. He shows quite logically how **Spirit** apparently exercised **selection** by deciding that there shall be a formed universe, and controlled the **selection** of the details of creation.

In addition to the power of **selection, Spirit** possesses the power of **initiative.** It **initiates** the **Creative Sequence** by its "Let there be," and releases its Word completely to **Mind** the Builder.

Mind obeys

Mind the Builder, **obediently** and without question, accepts the decree and proceeds to carry it out. **Mind** molds the plastic, unresisting, inert **Primary Unformed Substance** into the form of the idea expressed by **Spirit,** following with exactitude as though from a blueprint.

Mind is characterized by **obedience.** Its function in the **Creative Process** is to carry out unswervingly whatever **Spirit** selects for creation.

It possesses all knowledge. It knows how to construct a universe. It knows how to open the way into higher living, prosperity, health. It works with quiet certainty.

Yet it never originates its own plan. It must always work from the pattern given it. It is always **obedient.**

Body, Unformed Substance, is molded into form

Body, the **Unformed Primary Substance** — inert, insubstantial — is molded into form, and becomes a universe. **Body** is completely subservient to any action **Mind** makes upon it. It is easily moldable into the form of rocks, trees, flesh, etc.

At this point, we might observe that the thought of **Spirit** does not "influence" **Body** to become a certain thing. Instead, the thought of **Spirit** actually becomes the form as unsolid steam becomes the form of ice.

Or, to use another illustration: A whirling airplane propeller seems invisible, insubstantial, becoming visible as a form only when it is slowed down. So it is with **Unformed Substance** becoming formed.

Spirit creates a thing by becoming it. By lowering that which **Spirit** has selected (invisible) to a visible level (form), **Mind** completes the **Creative Cycle.**

Mind the Builder, or Fabricator, takes the original, identical idea, or concept, of **Spirit** and condenses it down into actual form.

Thus the form is the original idea lowered into visibility to us. It was just as real when it was only a concept. We humans, living in a world of sense, make the mistake of thinking it is real only when our sense organs can apprehend it.

Physicists say that all matter is nothing but **force** condensed into form, and that electricity is the point at which force is turning into form. They say that electricity (in the electron) is force at its densest point, and is matter at its least dense point.

The thoughts of **Spirit** and **Mind** are force; **therefore, it is quite conceivable that the entire universe is the thought of God in visible form.**

God is all — and in all

Since both **Force** and **Substance** have been present from the remotest beginning, coequal parts of the **Originating Intelligence,** it is quite logical to assume that the entire universe, including us, can rightly be called the **Body** of God.

From this point of view, there was originally nothing but God; there is still nothing but God though in changed form. God **is** all and **in** all. "In Him we live and move and have our being."

This is of the greatest importance, for the student who understands this most clearly will do the best work in treating for himself or others.

MAN ALSO IS A trinity OF spirit, mind, AND body

Man is in the small what God is in the large. Man is made in the image and likeness of the **Infinite** in that he has the power to create his own world.

Man, therefore, is **spirit (surface mind), mind (deeper mind),** and **body,** these three phases being characterized by the same qualities as those attributed to their **Counterparts.** This correspondence between man's **spirit, mind,** and **body** and those **Counterparts** in the **Infinite Trinity** refers to their mode of action.

(Refer constantly to the charts on the **Creative Process.** The more you study them, the more clearly you will see the **obedient** response of this vast **Creative Power** to your conscious choices.)

Surface mind selects and initiates

Psychologists tell us that there is one area of man's **mind** that has the power to **select** any objective it desires, and then to

57

initiate the necessary steps to bring that objective into being. Man's conscious mind, called in this course his **surface mind,** has the power to **select, initiate,** and decree what his **deeper mind** shall bring forth.

Man's **surface mind** corresponds to **Spirit** in the **Infinite Trinity.**

At this point, the student may ask, "How can this be, that man's **surface mind** corresponds to **Spirit? Spirit** is sinless, without spot or blemish, always resting in perfect peace. Man's **surface mind** is wicked, often devilish. I can't see this."

There is no contradiction here at all. Man is made in the image and likeness of God in that he possesses the qualities, traits, and abilities that enable him to create his own world of experience by the same process that created the universe. His **surface mind** corresponds to **Spirit** in its power to **select** and **initiate.** It is not so much the quality of man's thinking but the ability to **select** a course of action and to **initiate** the movement that fulfills it that makes man's **surface mind** the counterpart of **Spirit** in the **Originating Trinity. The power to choose is man's greatest power.**

Deeper mind obeys

Psychologists tell us further that man has an **obeying** phase of his **mind.** It does not reason, select, or initiate anything. It merely accepts the suggestions or the dictates of the **surface,** or reasoning, **mind,** and immediately proceeds to carry them out. It accepts and **obeys** any pattern set before it. (Herein lies the basis for all forms of suggestion or autosuggestion and hypnosis.)

Man's subconscious mind, called in this course his **deeper mind,** automatically **obeys** that which is passed on to it by his **surface mind.** It acts always in complete **obedience** to the decrees of his **surface mind.** It works ceaselessly turning the material of our thought into the experiences of our lives.

Man's **deeper mind** corresponds to **Mind** in the **Infinite Trinity.**

Body reflects man's thought

Just as the **Body** of the **Originating Intelligence** is the entire material universe, so the **body** of man is his entire environmental world, as well as his physical body. It is his family, home, work, possessions, and his physical body.

Man's physical body is molded and shaped by the combined action of **surface** and **deeper mind.** His home, business, and every area of his life are likewise a reflection of his thinking.

Man **selects** a goal in his **surface mind** and **initiates** the action, releasing it to **deeper mind,** which **obeys** the decree and acts upon **body** to bring it into form.

Each student has the power to reproduce the **Creative Process** in himself and his own affairs. He can use precisely the same **Creative Process** to bring about a change in his personal life as the **Infinite** used to bring a universe into being.

SPIRIT IS CAUSE — MIND IS CREATIVE MEDIUM

Spirit in the Trinity — the **Infinite** and the **finite** — is cause, as you see by the charts. Our choices originate in our **surface mind (spirit).** The action that brings them to pass is that of **deeper mind,** once we learn to release it to this only agent that can bring it to pass.

Mind in the Trinity — the **Infinite** and the **finite** — is creative medium, also as you see by the charts. It is the working phase of the Trinity. It carries within itself all the "know-how" of creation. It knows how to build a sun or a planet, a blade of grass or a redwood, a cell or a child. It knows how to restore perfect structure and function in a body. It knows how every successful business was ever built, and how any person ever drew love and companionship into his life. Its knowledge is absolutely without limit; it is omniscient. Yet it is dedicated to the will of man in creating his own world. **Deeper mind** will carry out to completion any pattern that **surface mind** keeps at the focus of attention, and it will do it easily, effortlessly.

Spirit in the **Infinite, surface mind** in the individual, **decides** what it wants done, and, as it were, says, "Let there be" (release), thus passing the action onto **Mind** or **deeper mind,** which is dedicated always to obey **Spirit** or **surface mind,** and carries out the order.

But there is nothing inferior about the place **Mind** or **deeper mind** holds in the Trinity. It is not a slave. It is simply the working phase of the Trinity.

Genesis describes the Creative Process

The Old Testament story of creation may seem crude and naive because it was set down in a day long before scientific findings in this field; yet it is remarkable how those ancient seers "felt" their way to scientific truths, and stated them in terms whose significance they probably did not fully grasp.

When they wrote, "And God said, let there be light; and there was light," they were describing this **Creative Cycle — Spirit selecting** and **initiating** the movement by "Let there be"; **Mind obeying,** swinging into action, applying its "know-how"; "and there was light."

It should be apparent now that the Science of Mind does not depart from the Bible, but reinterprets it in the light of modern knowledge.

SPIRIT HAS THE POWERS OF
SELECTION AND INITIATIVE

Universal creation gives evidence of **choice,** or **selection,** by the fact that it is not universe wide, but occurs in spots. What caused stars to be built at intervals? There is no scientific answer to this, but it is an indication of the power of **Spirit, Originating Intelligence,** to **select** spots for creation; and so we can assume that one of the characteristics of **Originating Intelligence** is the power of **selection.**

But there must be an additional power, for the ability to **select** without a concomitant power to carry out the **choice** would have left **Spirit** the prisoner of its own imaginings. The very fact that creation was carried into form indicates, then, that **Spirit** has the power to **select,** then to **initiate** in its **Mind**-phase the action that brings into manifestation that which **Spirit** has **selected.**

We continue to repeat that one of the fundamentals in the Science of Mind is that man's **surface mind** has the powers of **selection** and **initiative.** If man had only the ability to **select** and not the ability to **initiate,** he would be tantalized beyond endurance, always tormented by desire, yet without the power to attain. Fortunately, the **Creative Process** will work unfalteringly for man just as it did for **Originating Intelligence.**

Each student can select **a goal to be demonstrated before the completion of this course; he can then** initiate **the action in the Creative Cycle by speaking his word, that is, by declaring its fulfillment;** and he can go forward in the conviction that he can reach that goal — not in some far-off heaven beyond the grave, but here and now in his earth existence.

Progress comes from using selection and initiative

All man's advances have come through his power of **choice.** The rise from barbarism to civilization has been a repeated going on from one **selection** to a better one. But the power of **selection** has been exercised by comparatively few. The great masses, sunk in mental lethargy, have scarcely dreamed that there might be something higher and better. Thus they have been content with things as they have found them, things that their leaders have **selected** for them.

The thinkers of the race, filled with a "Divine Discontent," have always **chosen** to seek the higher levels. In the material life, our inventors have **selected** the better way of doing things, hence our advance from foot to horseback to automobile and airplane; from pounding a shirt with a block of wood in a running stream to our modern washing machine and laundromat; from smoke signals on a hilltop to radio and television.

Without the twin abilities to select **a better way and to** make it come true, **man today would still be living in a cave.**

MAN'S CONCEPT OF GOD IS GROWING

In the mental and spiritual field, man has had a **growing** conception of the **Infinite.** Daring souls have weighed the old, measured it against a new idea, **selected** the new, and have sometimes been killed for it. But later the masses have accepted the new ideas, and because of it have moved a step nearer to clear understanding. The twentieth-century view of God is no more like the cruel tyrant of the Dark Ages than the automobile is like the Roman chariot.

The most modern view of God is that of the Science of Mind, which appeals both to reason and to spiritual insight; and since it so definitely brings healing to all discordant conditions, it is evidently nearer the truth than the earlier conceptions, for "by their fruits shall ye know them."

It is comfortable to stay in a rut; it takes mental effort to get out. Unthinking people have always been angry when asked to pull free of their settled ignorance. Yet someone must pioneer, and when he does, usually he is accused of "doing away with God." No one can do away with God. He is quite able to look after Himself. The only thing the exploring thinker does away with is a superstitious concept of God. Much of the "Zeal for God" is only zeal for one's settled opinions.

Truth is inexhaustible, and the Science of Mind view is by no means the ultimate. It is the best we have today, but it will be further clarified to a still clearer truth by deeper study and understanding of our universe. When those clarifications come, they will do so through the ability of someone to **select** the greater in place of the lesser.

What is God's will?

Millions of persons today believe that it is the "will of God" that they should endure illness, poverty, unhappiness. They resign themselves to it because they do not know that they can **select** a better level of life and move onto it.

You, the student, are among the pioneers who emphatically reject this belief about the will of God. This course will enable you to prove to yourself and to others who are not blinded by prejudice that God's will for man is that he shall become more of himself, release more of his hidden powers, and draw more of his good to himself without hurting others in their search for their own good.

WHY ILLNESS DEVELOPS IN MAN

Perhaps the student is now coming to see that sickness and other misfortunes develop in man because **deeper mind** is compelled to accept whatever thoughts are given it. It has no power of choice at all. It is an automatic receptor of the **choice** already made by **surface mind.** Whether it is constructive or destructive, **deeper mind** must carry out into form the thought of **surface mind.** The person who is always thinking, talking, or reading about symptoms and illness is actually saying, "Let there be illness." And **deeper mind** will **obey** his decree. He will become ill.

That person will indignantly deny this, of course, but that does not change the fact that with his mouth he may be pleading for health, but with his thought he is ordering illness. We are not always aware of the quality of our thought, and certainly do not notice the lightning speed of our **choices.** Once we have become habituated to negative thought, we automatically **choose** this kind, then believe it has forced itself upon us.

Surface mind MUST SELECT POSITIVE THOUGHTS

Every thought has two sides — the positive and the negative. Whenever a thought presents its discouraging side to us, we can know that its positive side is there also, waiting to be **selected.** For example, one cannot think of sorrow without also thinking of joy, because sorrow is the absence of joy. Illness is the absence of health. Poverty is the absence of prosperity. Failure is the absence of success. We can see now how highly important is this matter of **selection.**

Man's **deeper mind** is the seat of his emotions, his feelings. His **surface mind** is the seat of his reason, his **choices.** Neither can carry on the activities of the other. They remain forever separate and distinct to our human eyes.

Deeper mind depends on **surface mind** to protect it from error; but after the same **choice** has been made repeatedly, **deeper mind** comes to expect that sort of **choice** to be made; and once the thought has passed into its sphere, it goes to work on it, habitually fabricating it into form.

Thus negativity or positivity is nothing but a mental habit to which **deeper mind** has become accustomed and automatically expresses. The encouraging feature of this is that **deeper mind** is highly educable; it can be re-educated.

Through repeated **choice,** a certain type of thought becomes a feeling. The person who lives by his feelings alone can never control the **Creative Cycle,** because he is allowing the servant to become the master. **Deeper mind,** the feeler, must always remain the servant of **surface mind,** the **chooser.**

Reason and choice must control the feelings

There are three classes of persons who live by their feelings, or allow their feelings to dictate their actions. They are the savage, the child, and the insane — all unstable, undeveloped types. The mark of the civilized man is his ability to let reason and **choice,** not feelings, prevail.

The person who says, "I just don't feel like working today," and who acts on that feeling, is headed for failure. His mentally developed brother will say, "I don't feel like working today, but I simply must get to work." This man is using **choice** and **initiative,** and is thus setting in action the **Creative Cycle** for a definite purpose. By the end of the day, he will have produced something worth while.

On waking up "blue"

People quite often say, "I really intend to start thinking and acting positively; but when I wake in the morning, it seems as if a wave of gloom sweeps over me. I just can't get started." Many people often feel this way, but, while we cannot help it if the birds fly over our house, we can keep them from building nests in the eaves; and the way we do this is through **selection** and **initiative.**

The first thing upon awakening, **choose** to slant the mind in the direction of the good. The slanting may be done in many ways. One student has found it helpful to say, "I wonder what nice experience I'll have today, what pleasant people I'll meet, what good business I'll do, what nice contacts I'll make." It has revolutionized her life.

Deeper mind can be re-educated

Cultivate the expectancy of the good, and do it deliberately. If a myriad **choices** of the bad have gradually slanted the mind into a negative pattern, faithfully follow through with the practical application for each lesson, particularly the thought training, and establish a new, positive pattern. And remember that even though one has thought negatively for forty years, it does not take forty years to overcome that habit. Remember the farmer's horse in Lesson 2.

One constructive thought is more powerful than ten thousand destructive thoughts, because constructive thought is in line with the thinking of the Originating Intelligence, **and, therefore,** has **superlative force.**

Start every morning in the way the student above did. It will pay real dividends, for you will find that you are on your way to a life in which your feelings will come to back up your **choices,** not determine them.

Thus we can change from bad thought-habits to good ones, from a pessimistic disposition to an optimistic one. Once we begin to take this way of the **Creative Process** in the individual, we can make ourselves what we want to be.

The next lesson will deal further with Body, the third phase of the Trinity.

SPECIAL HELPS IN STUDY
AND PRACTICAL APPLICATION

These special helps have been carefully prepared to help you to get the most out of this course.

Questions on the lesson

I advise that you first study the lesson carefully, then put it aside, write the answers to the questions, and, finally, **check your answers by the lesson.**

Keep the answers as a running commentary on the course **for your own benefit.** At its conclusion, you will find they have become a record of your own growth in consciousness.

1. What is the significance for us that there is only one **Creative Process?**

2. What must have been the source of the energy that created the universe?

3. Explain fully and clearly by means of a chart the threefold nature of the **Infinite.**

4. Explain fully and clearly by means of a chart, "Man is in the small what God is in the large."

5. Explain concisely the way man can use the **Creative Process.**

6. Exactly what is meant by the characteristics of **selection** and **initiative?**

7. What is the basis of all progress, and what is the great significance of this for man?

8. What is the explanation for illness and other unwanted conditions in one's life?

9. What are some practical ways in which **surface mind** can do its part?

10. Why can we say that one constructive thought is more powerful than ten thousand destructive thoughts?

Collateral reading suggestions

Please continue to keep in mind my comments on these suggestions as I gave them in Lesson I.

Frederick Bailes: "Your Emotions Can Kill or Cure"
Your Mind Can Heal You, Ch. I (1941)
Ch. II (1971)

Bessie Beihl: The Lord Is **Your** Shepherd

Thomas Troward: The Creative Process in the Individual, Ch. II

Practical application

. . . thought-training

Follow the suggestion in the latter part of the lesson each morning.

Choose that immediately on awakening you will deliberately turn your thought toward the expectancy of something good.

. . . writing suggestion

Write at least seven positive statements that you can use to turn your thoughts in the right direction when you find them dwelling on things that you do not want in your life.

. . . a treatment for general good

I know that my word is the word of power.

I definitely speak my word to set **Infinite Law** into action.

It follows the **Perfect Pattern** in my body, my business, my personal relationships.

I shall be a blessing to everyone I meet this day.

I know that I can meet any experience successfully, that I neither fear nor expect evil.

I now fill my horizons with the expectancy of the good.

I will live expectantly, knowing that my good awaits me at every point and at every minute this day.

I know that I will dwell in the sunlight of the **Healing Presence** forever.

I declare this to be the truth for all whose hearts are tuned to right action this day.

And it **is** so.

Lesson 5

WHY MAN'S MIND IS CREATIVE
(continued)

THREEFOLD NATURE OF THE INFINITE
    (continued from page 48)

BODY, UNFORMED SUBSTANCE, is molded into form
    (continued from page 56)

MAN ALSO IS A trinity OF spirit, mind, AND body
    (continued from page 57)

Body reflects man's thought
    (continued from page 58)

— illness begins in the thought
— changed thought produces changed conditions

TO MIND THERE ARE NO INCURABLE ILLNESSES
Why some conditions seem incurable

CONSCIOUSNESS IS THE KEY TO HEALING
Consciousness of GOODNESS
Consciousness of BEAUTY
Consciousness of INFINITY
Consciousness of LOVE
Consciousness of HARMONY

TREATMENT IS NEVER A PETITIONING PRAYER

ALL CREATION IS THE SELF-CONTEMPLATION OF SPIRIT
Spirit sees perfection; man sees imperfection

PURPOSE OF TREATMENT — TO HEAL THE FALSE BELIEF

67

FIFTH LESSON
GOALS

To come into a still clearer understanding
of why man's **mind** is creative

To make definite progress in cultivating
the healing consciousness

In our study of the **Creative Process** in the last lesson, we were concerned chiefly with the first two phases of the threefold nature of the **Infinite** (God) and of man — **Spirit** and **surface mind, Mind** and **deeper mind.** In this lesson, we shall talk about the third phase. Please refer to the segments of the charts marked **Body** in the **Infinite** and **body** in the individual.

THREEFOLD NATURE OF THE INFINITE
(continued from page 48)

BODY, UNFORMED SUBSTANCE, is molded into form
(continued from page 56)

The student should study the evidence until he is convinced that the **Body** of the **Infinite** refers to the entire manifest universe; likewise, the **body** of man refers to his physical body, his home, work and other material interests.

MAN ALSO IS A trinity OF spirit, mind, AND body
(continued from page 57)

Body reflects man's thought
(continued from page 58)

Just as the **Body** of the **Infinite** is the entire manifest universe, so the **body** of man is his entire personal world — his physical frame, material possessions, work, home, family. These constitute his world of effect.

His physical body and all the material aspects of the rest of his **body** are characterized by **inertia.**

It is quite evident, then, that man's physical body, being characterized by **inertia,** can, of itself, neither produce nor heal a disease, nor can it make any other change within itself. It is forever played upon by the images of his thought. Separated from **mind,** it can do nothing.

The arm moves because **mind** tells it to move. Severed from the body in which the **mind** operates, it cannot move. It will lie **inert** until it slowly disintegrates unless some force outside itself acts upon it. A foot can kick it; a table on which it lies may be shaken; a strong wind may blow against it — these outside forces can move it. But of itself, it cannot move because of its inherent **inertia.** In this, it is like any other piece of **inert** matter — a rock, for instance, which will stay where it is unless some outside force moves it.

In similar manner, the severed arm could not develop a disease, as can the arm on a living person. It could only disintegrate. In order to become diseased, the arm must be attached to a body through which **mind** operates.

Thought is the molder of the body. Man's physical body is **Substance.** When we think of bodily healing, it is imperative that we remember that **Substance** has no power to resist being molded into form, because that is exactly what does happen during a healing. The old form passes away; a new form is created under the activity of **deeper mind,** which is in and of **Infinite Mind.**

It should give the student courage to know that body cannot decide to stay ill when **surface mind decides** it shall become well. **Deeper mind** has irresistible power to heal the body; therefore, we speak our healing word with authority.

— illness begins in the thought

Body is always acted upon by something other than itself. Man's brain is a dynamo of power. Here are generated those currents of nerve energy that flow over the vast and intricate network of nerves to every part of the body.

Each individual cell is indwelt by **Intelligence,** but the **Intelligence** is not of itself, and it is not a reasoning intelligence. A cell separated from the body within which **mind** operates shows no intelligent action. The cells of the body must accept the **thought**-patterns of the person of whom they are a part.

Wave after wave of **thought** flows from the brain every moment we live. The **thought** is of either a constructive or a destructive nature. It colors every cell through which it passes, imparting its own quality to the cell.

Thus the person whose dominant strain of **thought** is that of anxiety, inward pressure, and irritation will eventually find the tissues of his body showing these patterns. In most instances, it shows up in the stomach cells, which seem more easily irritated than those of other organs. That irritation, if allowed to continue unchanged, can show up as gastritis, which is irritation of the stomach lining. If this is not sufficient to cause the person to change his **thought**-patterns, it can eventuate as stomach ulcers.

— changed thought produces changed conditions

It is well known that the physical means for dealing with ulcers have not been highly successful. Surgery has been done in which that portion of the stomach involved has been excised; yet in a few years many such patients have been back for more surgery. All the surgeon's knife had done was remove the **effect;** the **cause** of the ulcers had been left untouched. Various bland diets produce only temporary relief. When they are discontinued, the ulcers come back, because, as in surgical cases, the **cause** has not yet been dealt with.

On the other hand, there are thousands of cases on record in which, without either surgery or diet, ulcer patients have been completely restored to health through a changed mental and emotional attitude.

Sufferers say, "I could be happy if it were not for my stomach." The fact is, the stomach could be happy if it were not for the person. The cells of the body really enjoy ease, not dis-ease. We might become facetious for a moment and picture two stomach cells talking together. The one says, "I wish that fellow upstairs would stop being mad at everybody. I'm burning up down here." The other replies, "Yes, and he's the one who's always telling his friends what a burden **we** are to **him.**"

TO MIND THERE ARE NO INCURABLE ILLNESSES

Because of the **Principle** of **inertia,** there are **no incurable illnesses.** Body will readily move in any direction in which the mental currents are directed. But since people do not know this, sickness reigns and the sufferers blaspheme God by saying that He, for some inscrutable reason, imposes illness upon them. **God never lays sickness upon anyone.** Man brings it upon himself, and he can get rid of it as soon as he is willing to deal with it intelligently.

I speak from experience, for in 1915 I was condemned to die of diabetes. But I learned that the body is the sounding board of the mind, and that man's mental attitudes become his physical tissues. Insulin had not been used for the relief of this condition in 1915, or I assuredly would have begun taking it, for I was medically minded then, just finishing my training in London Missionary School of Medicine and London Homeopathic Hospital for what was to have been my lifework as a medical missionary. Had insulin been available at that time, it is highly probable that this course and many books on the Science of Mind would never have been written, and the progress of this truth would have been delayed by that much at least.

As encouragement to anyone who has not had immediate results from his changed viewpoint, may I point out that it was some years before I was completely sugar free. I could have been healed instantaneously had my understanding been complete, but in the beginning I knew very little of the Science of Mind, and the **Infinite** can do for us only what it can do through us at any stage of our unfoldment. My reading of Troward's **The Creative Process in the Individual** gave me my first glimpse of the relationship between **spirit, mind,** and **body.** As I gradually mastered the **Principles** of the **Creative Process,** my body gradually responded.

Why some conditions seem incurable

The body cannot refuse the dictates of **surface mind** even if it wanted to, which it certainly does not. Man has been deluded

71

in the past because certain diseases have been labeled "curable" and others "incurable." To **deeper mind,** nothing is incurable; and it knows no such terms as "hard" and "easy," "big" and "little," "serious" and "simple." One gets a pimple on the nose, laughs at it, and says, "It will be gone in a day or two." One day we shall come to the place where we can say the same thing of a malignancy, knowing it will be healed.

Of course we know that, from today's human and scientific point of view, the destructive processes at work in a malignancy are far more deadly than those in a pimple. Furthermore, they are not at all the same processes. But when we give spiritual treatment for those conditions, we must remember that we are dealing with a **Power** that is omniscient and omnipotent. Remember also that while human research has not yet uncovered a sure-fire method of treating malignancies, they have been healed by spiritual means from time to time down through the centuries as when Jesus brought about the healing of the woman with the "running sore." In these cases, human skill was by-passed, and the **Great Physician** called in. When **That-to-which-nothing-is-hidden** went to work, healing was the result.

Then why are not all malignancies healed? Because the human **mind** has been conditioned to the belief that some are incurable. None of us is aware of the race beliefs he carries in his **deeper mind** and of their intensity. But here and there is a person who breaks through the shell of the race thought and emerges into the clear light of **Infinite Mind.** When he does, the healing follows.

CONSCIOUSNESS IS THE KEY TO HEALING

It is natural that the student should be eager to learn the actual techniques of treatment. We have not yet gone into them at any length because the broad foundation we are endeavoring to lay is that of **consciousness.**

A high healing **consciousness** coupled with imperfect technique will produce more healings than a perfect knowledge of technique without the healing **consciousness.** The medical profession has sometimes been amazed when an unlettered person, perhaps one whose speech is atrociously ungrammatical, and who knows nothing of anatomy or physiology, has been able to produce sensational healings. The secret is **consciousness.**

The healing **consciousness** is not a gift vouchsafed to some fortunate persons. Anyone can cultivate it. It grows out of much thinking upon the bigness of the universe, the **Wisdom** and **Power** that guides the stars and the planets, the **Life** that works such beautiful veinings into the tiniest flower and puts the fragrance into the rose. I have treated for persons in distant lands whom I have known only by letter, and they have been completely healed by the healing **consciousness.**

Consciousness of GOODNESS

It grows out of a belief in the essential **Goodness** of human nature even when the acts of some individuals are vile, and out of a quality of universal love for all men. This latter is perhaps its most important ingredient.

Consciousness of BEAUTY

It is that in man that is enthralled by the rare beauty of a sunset, but that does not stop at the esthetic satisfaction of it, but goes further into a contemplation of **Absolute Beauty,** of which the sunset is only a tiny scintilla, and which is a quality in the nature of **Infinite Intelligence.**

Consciousness of INFINITY

It is that in man which, when he sits on a headland overlooking the vastness of the ocean, watching the steady rolling of waves as they tumble ashore, leads his thoughts on to that **Infinite Ocean of Mind,** of which his **mind** is a part, the **Ocean of Mind** that is powerful enough to sweep away the towering cliff of a malignancy as easily as it wipes out the sand pile of a pimple.

Consciousness of LOVE

The healing **consciousness** in man is that which knows that the highest expression of love he has ever seen — whether it be devotion between husband and wife, devotion of a mother for her spastic child, or devotion to country — is only the faintest shadow of some phase of **Infinite Love.** And since a river can rise no higher than its source, it also knows that if such heights of love are possible in earthly beings, then beyond and behind such human love there must be an **Infinite Love** without limit.

Consciousness of HARMONY

This course is being prepared at a beautiful spot high in the mountains of California, in the shade of a huge oak which has evidently seen the suns and snows of more than two hundred years, and from whose shade I have given healing treatment for thousands of men and women in all parts of the world. In the clean air is that quiet, lulling hum of mountains drowsing in the sun. As my nearest neighbor is almost half a mile away, there isn't a house nor any other sign of human being in sight.

A black and white retriever, which has adopted me, has followed me here and lies stretched at my feet in perfect relaxation. I hear the soft chatter of a squirrel, which has climbed the oak, and is looking down at me in friendly inquiry.

Birds in the surrounding trees are singing. Redheaded woodpeckers and gorgeous blue jays are bathing in the bird bath close by, and between times enjoying the bread crusts I have tossed there for them. More than a hundred mountain quail come each evening for the crushed grain I throw to them. These shy creatures come without fear, for I have no designs on them.

Scores of butterflies — yellow, cinnamon-brown, or white — flit about on their mysterious quests. And just now a flying insect, whose name I do not know, has made a landing on the rough board that is my desk. He is not more than three fourths of an inch long, brown, and shaped exactly like a prehistoric Brontosaurus, with a long, out-thrust neck, small snakelike head, and light-brown wings folded easily at his sides. He stays motionless, seemingly looking me over. He has no fear of me, even when I gently move my finger close to him. But presently, as if his curiosity has been satisfied, he spreads his wings and flies away.

In these beautiful natural surroundings, particularly at this peaceful moment when no creature seems to be afraid of any other creature, I feel one with the harmony of nature. And I can well understand that **Harmony** is a part of the nature of God. Seeking an analogy in music, I might say that all this is like a Grand Symphony to which many different instruments have contributed, each one blending its particular sound and appearance with the others to make up a harmonious whole.

It is not difficult, now, to move my thought on to harmony in the human body, which, as God fashioned it, is an expression of **Infinite Harmony.** This body is made up of many different parts, each with its particular function to perform, each actively looking out for itself, yet all functioning together for the good of the whole.

All this is **consciousness** of harmony; yet it is but the tiniest fragment of something far more vast that extends to the limits of the universe and beyond, for our universe has no limits, because it is the **Body** of God.

These are some of the ways in which students keep alive their high healing **consciousness.** No matter where one lives, there is always some secluded spot not far distant where he can be "alone with God," insulated from the bombardment of the world's thought. Even if he can get there only once a week, it will prove valuable.

The healing **consciousness** is much more, but those qualities mentioned may faintly indicate the difference between mere knowledge and **consciousness.** Later in the course we shall go further into the subject.

TREATMENT IS NEVER A PETITIONING PRAYER

Now, let us return to the charts in Lesson 4 illustrating the **Creative Process.** You will see that **Spirit is never acted upon.** This is why we, in the Science of Mind, do not use petition in our prayers. We never say, "Dear God, look upon this misery and get me (or this other person) out of it." Instead of petitioning, we **declare the truth** about ourselves or the other person, believing that it is the **truth that sets one free.**

One of the ancient writers said that God is "of purer eyes than to behold evil, and cannot look upon iniquity." That means that the universe must look entirely different to **Infinite Spirit** from what it looks to us. We, newcomers in it, see imperfections. **Spirit,** the **Originator,** sees it perfect as He made it.

ALL CREATION IS THE
SELF-CONTEMPLATION OF SPIRIT

Troward makes much of the fact that the **Originating Spirit** creates by **self-contemplation,** and that, since there is only one **Creative Process,** man creates in the same way, whether he knows it or not.

After picturing the **Originating Source,** the **Three-in-One,** Troward develops the idea that, since there was nothing else out of which a universe could have been constructed — there being only God and nothing — the only way in which things could have taken form must have been through the **Originating Being** thinking of itself, by self-contemplation, as being projected **as** the various forms in the universe.

It is notable that the world-famous physicist, Sir James Jeans, comes to the same conclusion. Jeans had gone into a search for the way in which this universe could have come into being. After having exhausted every possible physical hypothesis, he says:

> The universe can best be pictured as consisting of pure thought, the thought of what, for want of a better word, we must describe as a mathematical thinker.*

Since **Body** is part of the **Infinite Trinity,** as shown in the last lesson, it is evident that the universe would have to be produced out of that part of itself. It is quite conceivable, therefore, that **Spirit thought** of itself as being projected in form, as a universe, spun out of the **Universal Unformed Primary Substance;** that it **thought** of itself as being projected in the various forms we now see.

So **Creation** was the act of **Spirit contemplating** itself in a certain form or state of being, and **Mind,** always **obedient, fabri-**

* Rede Memorial Lectures, Cambridge, November 4, 1930

cating the universe in accordance with **Spirit's** thought-pattern. The **Creative Process,** or **Cycle,** was then completed. Science has no other satisfactory explanation.

Spirit, seeing itself as a certain thing, becomes that thing, and that which **Spirit** sees is always the **Good.** It is interesting to note that the writer of Genesis "feels" his way to a similar conclusion. He says, "And God saw everything that He had made, and behold, it was very good." This is the essence of the **self-contemplation** of **Spirit.**

Man as **spirit (surface mind)** likewise creates by **self-contemplation.** "As a man thinketh in his heart, so is he." Whatever man is conscious of being, he becomes, for **deeper mind** (subconscious mind) always obedient, **fabricates** his thought into the stuff of his affairs.

If one's most vivid **self-contemplation** is of his illness, **deeper mind** cannot **fabricate** health; if of his poverty or loneliness, **deeper mind** cannot **fabricate** prosperity or companionship. Luck or favoritism does not enter in; it is the inexorable working of **Cause and Effect. Deeper mind** is of a singular neutrality. It makes no independent judgments. It has no will of its own except to **obey** what is fed into it.

Spirit sees perfection; man sees imperfection

Spirit, then, always sees things as they really are — perfect. That is why **Spirit** is never acted upon by man. Man, seeing through the warped vision of the senses, beholds illness, grief, misery, in the very same place where **Spirit** sees itself in perfect form.

This is why our statement, "There is nothing to heal," is so difficult for some people to understand. What we mean is this: The only thing to heal is the false approach and the false belief, for all is **Spirit** in form; therefore, all is good, all is perfect.

It is man's perspective as regards the universe that makes him doubt this. It is somewhat similar to what we had in the old-time motion-picture theaters. Seated down front and off to the side, we saw the actors on the screen all out of perspective — long pipestems for legs, long narrow heads. If that were all we had ever known about motion pictures, we never should have gone back again. But someone takes us to the center of the theater or, better still, up into the operator's booth, from which the images are thrown on the screen; then we see the images as they really are — beautiful, perfectly proportioned.

In the present stage of his development, man finds himself sitting away off to the side. If he could, as it were, step up and look over God's shoulder, he would see things as they actually are; then he would know why we say, "There is nothing to heal except a false belief."

PURPOSE OF TREATMENT — TO HEAL THE FALSE BELIEF

Treatment is for the purpose of bringing our thought "up into the operator's booth" to heal our false **belief** of distortion. This is why we so often say that we do not treat the body as such; we treat the underlying **belief.** The student must get this important point clear in his mind; otherwise, he will find himself treating effects rather than **causes.**

When a condition is intelligently treated for and healed through spiritual methods, it can never return, because the false **belief** that supported it has been destroyed.

If a condition is removed only temporarily, it is a sign that our treatment has been only on the psychological level, or the level of suggestion or hypnosis. Many of the conditions removed through psychological treatment return. The reason is this: the conditions were removed by the mind of the psychologist, and when his mind let go of the patient, there was a recurrence; whereas, when we come to the lessons on treatment, we shall see that we form the picture, then we **release** it to **Infinite Mind,** which never slumbers nor sleeps, which is all-powerful, and which holds it to the end of the **Creative Cycle.**

Now the student can see why a person's whole manner of life enters into his treatment. We should also recognize that thoughts that **cause effects** that we do not want are not only those that are actively directed against other people and things — such as hatred, ill will, criticism, resentment — but also passive thoughts such as anxiety, fear, sorrow, frustration, disappointment, overload, inadequacy. Our life is an expression of our deepest **beliefs.** Even our unexpressed **beliefs** color our consciousness and become our thought-atmosphere. To heal the body or the business, one must heal the **belief.** To heal the **belief,** one must understand the importance of **selection** and **initiative** and their place in the **Creative Cycle.**

1. First, the **intelligence selecting;**
2. then, the **intelligence initiating** the cycle by "Let there be";
3. then, the action passing over into **deeper mind,** which does the work, and which
4. moves upon **body,** through **Law,** to follow the pattern selected.
5. **Body,** thus acted upon, is molded into the desired form.

All this grows out of a changed **belief.**

77

SPECIAL HELPS IN STUDY
AND PRACTICAL APPLICATION

These special helps have been carefully prepared to help you get the most out of this course.

Questions on the lesson

I advise that you first study the lesson carefully, then put it aside, write the answers to the questions, and, finally, **check your answers by the lesson.**

Keep the answers as a running commentary on the course **for your own benefit.** At its conclusion, you will find they have become a record of your own growth in consciousness.

1. What do we mean by the "**Body** of God" and the "**body** of man"?

2. What is the great significance in healing of the fact that man's physical body is characterized by **inertia?**

3. What is the molder of the body?

4. Why can we say that there are no incurable conditions?

5. When results are not forthcoming when we think they should be, what attitude should we take?

6. What underlies all healing?

7. How can one proceed definitely to cultivate a healing consciousness?

8. How does knowing that **Spirit** is never acted upon affect the way in which we pray?

9. What does the statement "There is really nothing to heal" mean to you?

10. What does treatment do?

Collateral reading suggestions

As usual, please keep in mind my comments on these suggestions as I gave them in Lesson I.

Frederick Bailes: "Healing the 'Incurable' "
Your Mind Can Heal You, Ch. VI

Thomas Troward: The Creative Process in the Individual, Ch. II

Practical application

. . . thought-training

Raise your consciousness of healing by meditating on the activities and manifestations of the **Infinite** named in this lesson.

. . . writing suggestion

Write your own version of "The Universe Is a Grand Symphony" or "Harmony Is the Keynote of the Universe."

. . . treatment for general good

This day I seek the consciousness of the **Infinite Presence,** so near and warm that it seems "closer than breathing, and nearer than hands and feet."

It is a steadying influence that says, "Lo, I am with you always."

The **Infinite Companion** is mine.

I draw inwardly upon the unseen currents of **Power** that flood my entire being.

Infinite Wisdom is my inner teacher, and becomes a lamp unto my feet and a light unto my path.

The **Infinite Healing Presence** steals silently throughout my entire body and through all my affairs.

It knows nothing of ugliness, for it is **Beauty.**

It knows nothing of illness, for it is **Health.**

It knows nothing of limitation, for it is **Abundance.**

My body, my business, my home, are saturated with the **Presence** this day.

And it **is** so.

Lesson 6

THE SENSE OF AUTHORITY

SIXTH LESSON
GOALS

To know clearly the foundation
for authority

To make definite progress in gaining
a sense of authority in treatment

One of the trends of modern science is in the direction of spiritualizing matter. A modern scientist would say that matter is composed of force expressed as electrons — positive and negative charges of electricity. In the Science of Mind, we use other words to say the same thing: that matter is **Spiritual Substance,** or the **Substance of Spirit.** Our **bodies are Spiritual Substance** condensed into form; and, being in the small what God is in the large, we are more than **body;** we are also **mind** and **spirit.**

THE FOUNDATION FOR AUTHORITY

In the two preceding lessons, we discussed the **Threefold Nature of Being,** the three phases of the One God:

Spirit — which, by thought, **selects, initiates,** and says, "Let there be."

Mind — which always **obeys** and knows how to bring into manifestation the desire of **Spirit** — and does so.

Body — which is the **inert Spiritual Primary Substance** upon which **Mind** acts, condensing it into the form of the thing that **Spirit** has selected and decreed.

Since this is not a course on religion, we discussed the **Threefold Nature of Being,** not for theological reasons, but to find a practical explanation of our own thought processes so that we may follow scientific thinking for the healing of our adverse conditions.

This sums up the one **Creative Process** as set forth by Troward, the process used by God to create the universe, which is His **Body.** It is likewise the process used by man, whether he is aware of it or not to create his world, including the condition of his material body and all his circumstances and affairs.

We have seen that the paramount thing in this **Creative Process** is **thought.** We shall now see further how this applies to the healing of the physical body.

Thought actually becomes form

It must be remembered that **thought** not only influences form; it actually becomes form.

To the average student, this is something that will need explanation. "How," he will ask, "can dense matter emerge from immaterial **thought?** How can anything as solid as rock, for instance, be composed of the same substance as **thought** — the finer vibration of **Spirit?**"

We have developed the argument that the whole **Creation** was drawn out of **Originating Spirit.** If that is so, then in some way it must have already been present hidden within **Spirit.**

83

We could use the illustration of the three-segmented telescope. At first sight, it appears to be a single cylinder, but we pull out the second segment, then the third, both of which are part of its structure. This might appear astounding to a savage seeing it for the first time. It is only one; yet it is three, as he soon learns.

For the purpose of instruction, we may think of **Spirit** seeing itself as the first cylinder, then **Mind** emerging as the **Fabricator,** finally form **(Body)** being brought into view. As man sees it, this would be reversed. He sees **Body** first, then **Mind** emerging, and, finally, the innermost segment as **Spirit.**

The illustration is reluctantly used since it does not fully illustrate the **Creative Cycle** except from the standpoint of appearance.

We might also consider again this homely illustration from an earlier lesson. We know that true steam is invisible. That which we see a short distance from the kettle spout is a visible lowered condensation of the invisible steam emerging right at the spout. Lower its molecular vibration further by passing it through or over condenser coils, and this invisible steam will show up as water. Lower it still further in condensation by freezing, and it becomes hard, solid ice. All these different forms, from invisible steam to hard, solid ice, are due to changes in the vibration of the same substance brought about by the operation of natural law.

And it is by operation of **Creative Law** that **thought,** invisible and intangible, becomes the solid body of man.

Man's body is thought-energy in form

We say, then, that the body is a living thing composed of **thought.** Some of our scientists have called this universe itself "a living Presence," and have argued that every inorganic atom is alive in a certain way.

If a person continues to think of his body as a hard, solid object, it is understandable that his consciousness of healing it through **thought** will never be very strong. To dispel such an illusion, we shall take up the question from another angle.

Every moment man lives, he is building new cells to take the place of those that are momentarily wearing out. Physiologists are now estimating that approximately a **million** red blood cells alone disappear and are replaced by new ones each **second.** When we multiply that by the other parts of the body, we see that the total number that drop out and are replaced in a single second — not to mention an hour or a day or any other longer period of time — is enormous.

And every single one of those cells is built under either a negative **thought**-pattern or a positive **thought**-pattern; for, just as the **thought** of the **Originating Intelligence,** falling into form, became the universe, so man's **thought,** falling into form, becomes his body. Thus it is not a question of man's intangible weak **thought** bombarding his hard flesh in an endeavor to change it; it is a matter of man's **selecting** the highest grade of health-**thought** possible so that this, falling into form, will become a healthy body.

The body is constantly being rebuilt. It is not the same even from one moment to the next.

We used to be told that the body is renewed every seven years. Then some authorities began to believe that it is built anew every seven to fourteen months. Now atomic science has been the means of giving us definite proof of its renewal. Dr. Paul C. Aebersold, when head of the Atomic Energy Commission, said in a booklet titled **Atoms at Work** that most of the body, at least ninety-eight per cent of it, is replaced in one year.

There is no such thing as a chronic disease, but there are many chronic disease-thinkers. A diseased cell in a sick person must go to make room for a new cell. What, then, creates a new diseased cell to take the place of the worn-out one that has gone? A continuance of the old destructive **thought**-pattern in what is called "cell-memory." That is all!

Thus it can readily be seen that one big obstacle to healing is removed.

EXTREMES OF THOUGHT
THAT DEFEAT ATTEMPTS TO HEAL

"But," says the self-doubting student, "I don't believe **my** thought is powerful enough to heal. I'm not a trained thinker; my education has been too limited. In addition, my will power is so weak I know I'd give up before my thought could influence my flesh."

When the student really comes to understand that the healing process does not involve his will power or struggle, but that the **Infinite Thinker** through his **thought** becomes flesh, his consciousness of healing will be greatly strengthened.

The student will gain further assurance when he comes to know that the **Infinite Mind** flows steadily and continuously through his brain at all times, and that **Infinite Mind** carries the memory of countless healings. He is now dealing, not with human frailty, but with **Absolute Power and Wisdom** — the **Power** and **Wisdom** that have never been balked or turned back, but have always accomplished their ends. We shall deal with this subject in more detail in a later lesson.

There are two extremes of thought to which the student may go, and both will defeat his attempts to heal. We have just mentioned self-depreciation — the low estimate of one's ability to accomplish his ends.

The other extreme is conceit — overwhelming self-esteem. It is evidence that the student has his mind on himself rather than on the tremendous **Power** of the **Infinite.** The person who says, "I am a powerful healer," has stepped out of the **Infinite** placement. He who says, "This is a marvelous **Law** of healing," will continue to heal.

It is noticeable that Jesus avoided both these extremes. He was fully aware, always, that the remarkable healings attributed to him were not accomplished by the human Jesus of Nazareth, son of Mary, but by the **Wisdom** of God that indwelt him. When the people would have lionized him, he said, "Of myself I can do nothing. It is the Father in me who doeth the work."

He also said, "I and the Father are one," because he knew that whatever God is in the large, he, Jesus, was in the small, and he knew that the selfsame **Power** that brought the world into being was working through him to bring new bodies to those who gathered about him for healing. It was his complete sense of oneness with the **Infinite** and with the **Infinite's** method of creating, and not self-aggrandizement, which prompted his statement, "I and the Father are one."

MAN IS AN EXTENSION OF INFINITE MIND

It is evident that Jesus considered himself an extension of the **Infinite.** He constantly kept his thinking in line with what he believed the eternal thinking to be. The oneness of which he spoke is a oneness of **thought** — the true oneness. And it was a practical oneness.

We said in an earlier lesson that man is an extension of the **Infinite** as the inlet is an extension of the ocean. Analyze a drop of ocean water and one from an inlet, and the same proportions of hydrogen and oxygen will be found in each. The inlet, though circumscribed by form, is still a part of the boundless ocean. In like manner, man, bounded by a body, is still a part of the **Infinite,** and is as eternal and indestructible. Man, "the drop," is in the small what God, "the ocean," is in the large.

Whatever is true of Infinite Mind is true of man

Man is an extension of **Infinite Mind;** therefore, whatever is true of that **Mind** is true of him. This is highly important.

Does the **Infinite** have **Power** to transcend every obstacle that might be thrown against it? Then so do we.

Does it have **Power** to bring anything to pass no matter how complex? Then so do we.

Does it rest always in quiet assurance of perfect **Peace** and **Harmony?** Then so can we.

Does it rest forever in the contemplation of **Beauty** of outer and inner? Then our minds too can always be filled with "those things that are beautiful, noble, and of good report."

Does it know that it can never be left stripped of its **Resources** because there is always a steady flow of all that is necessary for the fulfilling of life? Then so can we.

Does **Supply** flow like an endless river through every phase of the **Infinite?** Then so does it flow through all our affairs.

Man's true nature is the nature of God. When man believes himself less than this, he is believing an untruth. Thus, basically, man's troubles are the result of a false **belief. True healing, then, is the healing of this false belief.**

The consciousness of oneness gives power

Since man's true nature is nothing but an extension of the **Infinite,** it can be readily seen that what is called "oneness with God" must be oneness of thinking; that is, man thinking God's thoughts after Him.

This oneness of God and man is not hypothetical; it is actual. Man derives strength from his unified consciousness, unified with **Infinite Right Action.** When the personality becomes disintegrated, it is because that person sees two things: that which he desires, which the **Infinite** also sees; and an obstructing power that can block him from the attainment of his desire, which the **Infinite** does not recognize. The psychologist uses the term "frustration" for this double vision, and it is well known that frustrated persons are always unhappy persons who may become neurotic or worse.

Frustration will be unknown when man comes to understand that his true nature is **Divine,** an inheritance from, and an extension of, the **Infinite.** From his physical antecedents he inherits his physical form and characteristics. These constitute his physical, or outer, nature. From the **Infinite** he inherits a spotless **Perfection,** a life-giving **Power,** and an eternal **Wisdom** that can make him anything he wants to become. These constitute his true spiritual, or inner, nature.

It is a sign of man's bondage to the negative that he persistently ties himself to his human heritage and becomes one with it instead of uniting with his **Divine.** Frequently, we hear someone discussing a "family weakness" and excusing himself by saying, "My mother (or father) was always like that; so I suppose I came by it honestly."

The fact of the matter is that man's **Divine** qualities far outweigh his weak human heredity; and if he would continue to live as though he believed that "I and the Father are one," his human heritage would be very satisfactorily submerged.

TRANSCENDING THE PROBLEM IS HIGHLY IMPORTANT

In facing a weakness or any other problem, we have three possible courses to pursue. They are: Fight, Flight, and Transcendence.

Some persons fight with all their might against unwanted conditions; they fight furiously against those who oppose them. Then there are those who seek refuge from trouble in flight. Especially will they do this when it comes to their own weaknesses; they will never face them, or do anything to remove them or to improve themselves.

The Great Teacher neither fought nor ran away. He calmly rose in consciousness to the place where he could say, "The prince of this world cometh, and findeth nothing [no response] in me." Thus he **transcended** the problem.

There is a level of living where one does not have to control his anger, for anger is simply not there. If, when another viciously opposes or attempts to obstruct us, we get down on his level and fight, we unify with him. Oneness with the Father means to live in a mental world so far above the sordid level of our opponent that there is no point of contact with him. Only that which finds response in us can attach itself to us, and if nothing within us vibrates on the plane of discord and violence, these pass us by. It was on this highest level of **transcendence** that Jesus lived.

Of course, it is human nature (not **Divine**) to want to get even with those who have wronged us — to "tell them off." And humans are inclined to attribute this reaction to righteous indignation rather than to what it really is — the lower self finding an ego-satisfaction in retaliation, a satisfaction that is a very poor one. The highest satisfaction comes from knowing that "greater is he that is in you than he that is in the world."

The many people who think they are dealing with their problems by never asserting themselves are really only running away from them. There is the wife, for instance, who, in the presence of a bullying husband, will remain silent for fear of touching off a worse scene. And there is the person who becomes a doormat for employer or fellow employees because he will not face the realities of a situation. These persons give in when they should assert themselves.

It is one thing to give in from fear, and a totally different thing to refrain from forcing an issue because of a sense of mastery. The first is cowardice. The second is courage of the highest order. The latter was the sort of courage that gave Jesus his very positive attitude of **authority.**

Each of us houses two tenants — a larger and a smaller self. The smaller one is the self magnified by the world in general. We in the Science of Mind seek to magnify the larger self, and make that self "greater than he that is in the world."

Here, again, we exercise our power of **selection.** Man stands between his larger and smaller selves; he can hold out the hand to either the lesser or the greater self. When we **choose** the greater, we are meeting our problem by **transcending** it.

Destructive habits

We digress at this point to touch on something that will receive more complete treatment later on — the victory over destructive habits gained through **transcendence.** The Science of Mind way to free oneself from a bad habit is not to fight it, but to lose all desire for it. There is a higher state of consciousness than desire to quit the habit, or desire to master it, or desire to continue it. That state above all desire connected with it is the state where one is so occupied with the **Reality** of life as it pertains to his own person that everything less than the complete self does not exist. This is what we shall go into more fully later.

AUTHORITY COMES THROUGH KNOWING

In reading the life of Jesus, it is interesting to note how often the word **authority** was used concerning him. The people recognized a very real sense of **authority** in the way he spoke.

There is a difference in the power of a man's word when he really **knows** what he is talking about. The salesman who knows his goods, and also knows his competitor's so well that, if challenged, can give reasons why his are better — this man has an inward sense of **authority** that creates sales. The same is true of the speaker who really has had an experience of the truth he talks about.

The Great Teacher had penetrated into that quiet place in the unseen world where **spirit** with **Spirit** can meet; he had touched the **Infinite,** and grasped the underlying **Law** that makes man's thought potent. He had come to **know** certain things, not merely believe them. Thus he spoke with authority.

How to gain authority in treatment

There must be no uncertainty in treatment. The student must develop, within himself, such a clear concept of what goes on during a treatment that he has not the slightest doubt but that the manifestation will come. The prayers of many are nothing but an expression of their fears; therefore, they are not answered. The student's treatment must be a statement of his beliefs and of his **knowing,** because **knowing** is higher than believing.

He must **know** that when he treats, something begins to happen on the hidden side of life that was not happening before he treated, for a treatment is a definite movement of **Mind** in a definite direction to accomplish a definite end. He must come into a sure and certain knowledge that "my word shall not return unto me void, but it shall accomplish that which I please, and it shall prosper in the thing whereto I sent it." He can gain this certainty by becoming thoroughly familiar with these two facts:

    1. The complete **obedience** of his **deeper mind.**

    2. The readiness of the **Loom of Mind** to carry through into form those thoughts he feeds into it.

The beginning of a real sense of **authority** is to **know** that the **Law of Mind** is as **obedient** as the law of electricity.

CULTIVATE CONSCIOUSNESS ABOVE TECHNIQUES

It is hoped that the student has now come to see the very great importance of **consciousness.** Techniques can always be learned; **consciousness** is a matter of growth in the cultivation of certain inward attitudes. It is an unfoldment of the real person within.

Thousands of salesmen are buying courses in salesmanship and many of them wonder why their study of these does not lead them to produce a greater volume of sales. These courses teach the externals — the way to approach the prospect, how to arouse his interest, how to guide the interview towards a decision, and, at last, how to close the deal. But the big thing, that inner attitude which is, as it were, the gasoline that drives the engine, is too often missing.

I once taught a Realty Board in a large city a course in salesmanship. At the beginning, I explained that I was not going to teach them the mechanics of selling; they had completed several courses that had taught them that. I said I was going to try to impart to them those inner states of mind, the sales **consciousness,** that would be the actual deciding element in closing their sales.

At the conclusion of the course, I received a letter from the secretary of the Board saying that the men had agreed that my course was better than all the others they had taken, and that, as a result of taking it, every member of that class had reported not only larger sales but also cleaner sales.

Cultivate your inner **consciousness.**

Our next lesson will go into the technique of treatment.

SPECIAL HELPS IN STUDY
AND PRACTICAL APPLICATION

These special helps have been carefully prepared to help you get the most out of this course.

Questions on the lesson

I advise that you first study the lesson carefully, then put it aside, write the answers to the questions, and, finally, **check your answers by the lesson.**

Keep the answers as a running commentary on the course **for your own benefit.** At its conclusion, you will find they have become a record of your own growth in consciousness.

1. What is the foundation for authority?

2. What bearing does this have on our attitudes toward the healing of the physical body?

3. What should be our attitude toward our physical body?

4. What extremes of thought defeat attempts to heal?

5. Explain the relationship of man's **mind** to **Infinite Mind.**

6. What is the great significance of this for man?

7. What are the values of transcendence over the other ways of meeting problems?

8. Explain "Authority comes through knowing."

9. How can we gain a sense of authority in treatment?

10. What is the difference between technique and consciousness in treatment?

Collateral reading suggestions

Please continue to recall my comments on these suggestions as I gave them in Lesson I.

Frederick Bailes: Hidden Power for Human Problems,
                       Ch. 11

                              Your Mind Can Heal You, Ch. VIII

Ervin Seale: Learn to Live

Practical application

. . . thought-training

Turn your thoughts to increasing your consciousness that whatever is true of **Infinite Mind** is true also of you.

Use the ideas in the section "Whatever is true of **Infinite Mind** is true of man" to direct your thoughts.

. . . writing suggestion

Write out some definite ways by which you are going to increase your sense of authority in treatment.

. . . a treatment for general good

This day I seek a deeper understanding of myself.

I know that I am part of the **Infinite Intelligence.**

It is ageless; therefore, I know that eternal currents of tireless energy flow through every cell of my body this day.

It is perfect; therefore, there is no room in me for that which is called illness.

It is **Life;** therefore, nothing destructive can operate to my hurt.

It is **Wisdom;** therefore, my thought has balance so that I am guided in all right action this day.

It is **Fullness;** therefore, my cup of blessing overflows.

This day I am alive to my true nature, the visible expression of that **Eternal Good** that is forever invisible, which worketh in me to will and to do of its good pleasure.

And it **is** so.

Lesson 7

THE TECHNIQUE OF TREATMENT

BASIC ESSENTIALS
What a treatment is
The practitioner works with his own thought only
In treatment, talk about the patient, not to him
How often to treat
Every treatment a unit

THE REALIZATION METHOD

THE ANALYTICAL, OR REASONING, METHOD

THE SEVEN "R'S"

FIRST "R" — RELAXATION
Physical relaxation
Mental and emotional relaxation
— imperfect persons can treat successfully
— cleanse the inner life
— the whole life goes into the treatment

SECOND "R" — RECOGNITION

OMNIPOTENCE — ALL POWER

OMNISCIENCE — ALL KNOWLEDGE

OMNIPRESENCE — EVERYWHERE PRESENT

(continued in the next lesson)

SEVENTH LESSON
GOALS

To understand the technique of treatment as so far given

To make definite progress:

In increasing your mental and emotional relaxation

In expanding your concept of

Omnipotence
Omniscience
Omnipresence

The most successful healer who ever lived was Jesus. In his discourses, he laid out clearly the fundamental **Principles** that underlie all successful treatment; yet there is no record that he ever outlined the technique of treatment. This has been left for a modern age to discover and set forth.

Different practitioners have different methods of treatment, but they fall into two main divisions — the Realization Method and the Analytical Method. The first is probably the one most frequently used by Jesus although there is evidence that at times he also used the other.

Before beginning our discussion of the particular methods, we shall give some general essentials underlying either method.

(Since from now on, we shall use the term "practitioner" frequently, it will be well to explain that by it we mean anyone who practices the Science of Mind in his daily living.

(We use the term "patient" throughout this course in spite of the fact that it has been used almost exclusively in medical practice. The original meaning of the word is "one who suffers." It can, therefore, be applied to one who suffers from loss or loneliness or frustration or defeat in any phase of his experience. Some professional practitioners of the Science of Mind refer to their patients as "students" or "clients.")

BASIC ESSENTIALS

What a treatment is

A treatment consists of the formulation of a concept of perfection, accompanied by a conviction of its truth with the assurance that the **Creative Law of Mind,** through **Omniscience, Omnipotence,** and **Omnipresence,** invariably proceeds to translate it into form.

In simpler language, a treatment is the releasing of our highest thought about a person or a condition with the assurance that **Infinite Creative Mind** begins immediately to bring to pass that which we have embodied in the treatment.

The practitioner works with his own thought only

At the outset, it must become clear to the student that, whichever method he is using, he is not trying primarily to influence the thought of the patient directly. What he does will eventually affect the patient's thought, but the purpose of the treatment is to keep the practitioner's own thought free from the patient's erroneous belief, and to convince the practitioner himself of the truth about the patient, which is that he is a perfect manifestation of the **Infinite,** and that whatever is true of the **Infinite** is necessarily true of the patient. The entire treatment is an action

within the mind of the practitioner, **by** himself, **upon** himself, but for the purpose of correcting the patient's false belief. It is highly important that the practitioner see this clearly.

The practitioner knows that poverty, illness, and other adverse conditions manifesting in the realm of the physical are only distorted **thoughts** that have taken form. He deals with them primarily.

If, for instance, he is treating the sick, he remembers that man thinks, not alone with his brain, but with every single cell of his body; therefore, the illness is one of **thought,** the manifestation one of form. Thus he knows that the healing must be a healing of the destructive **thought,** and that this will result in a healed body. The latter will be called the healing by some, but the practitioner knows that it is only the outer manifestation of the **real inward healing.**

The practitioner sees the body not as flesh and bones, hard and unyielding, but as **Spiritual Substance,** whose form can be changed as easily as one would alter the form of a rising column of smoke by a slight movement of the finger through it. This realization enables him to hold the conviction of the alterability of the physical. As soon as his conviction concerning the patient is clear, without doubt or mental reservation, the treatment is complete.

The treatment, therefore, is an operation of **Mind** that begins and ends in the **thought** of the practitioner; its fruits will be shown in the patient.

In treatment talk about the patient, not to him

When one treats for another, the words in either method of treatment are always spoken in the third person, never in the second. We do not say, "You are well"; we say, "John Smith is well." The former tends toward hypnosis or suggestion; the latter is a statement of the truth that we believe concerning John Smith, who has been entertaining a false belief about himself.

When we treat for ourselves, we use the first personal pronoun — "I," "me," "my," "mine."

How often to treat

It is best to give treatment two or three times a day, always making sure to **release** the treatment to **Infinite Mind,** for it is "the Father who doeth the work." If we find ourselves coming back too often to treat again, it is a sign that we have not properly and completely **released** it.

The way to **release** will be given in the next lesson.

If we are sure that "He is able [and willing] to keep that which I have committed unto Him," we shall make a complete

release. The Infinite never forgets; we have other things to divert our attention, but we can rest assured that the **Infinite** still carries that which we have committed unto it, and is changing the form accordingly.

If, therefore, we are tempted to treat too often, we merely touch the treatment lightly with our thought, as the child touches the hoop he rolls down the street after he has given it the initial movement. We say to ourselves, ''Well, I'm glad **Infinite Mind** is working for John Smith.'' This is what we mean by ''touching lightly.''

Every treatment a unit

Let every treatment be as though it were the only treatment that we are going to give for that person. When we give another at the end of the day, let it be as though we were starting again at the beginning.

Never let the idea of time to enter in. Do not say or think, ''This is serious, and therefore will probably take a long time to heal.'' Remember that we are dealing with limitless **Power** that can heal instantly, and would always heal instantly except for the barrier of our ''time'' thought or some other obstruction in the human consciousness.

Even when the practitioner finds it necessary to continue treatment for some weeks or months before the patient gives complete response, he gives each treatment as if it were the first and only one given.

The moment improvement shows, give thanks. Say, ''That's good, **Infinite Mind,** I know you're on the job.''

THE REALIZATION METHOD

The Realization Method is the simpler of the two methods. As its name implies, it is that movement of **Mind** by which we come instantly and simultaneously to a **realization** of the following:

    1. The nothingness of the condition

    2. The unchanged **Perfection** that lies beneath the apparent ugly surface condition

    3. The **Omnipotence** of the **Power** that is directed toward the patient

    4. The undeviating **obedience** of the **Law of Mind** that responds to the thought of the practitioner

In using the Realization Method to treat for another, the practitioner would say, either audibly or to himself, something like the following:

John Smith is the offspring of the **Infinite;** he partakes of the **Divine** nature, structure, and quality. This distorted condition is only the shadowing forth of his disturbed and distorted views of life and of himself. These thoughts are merely his beliefs.

I refuse to accept his false concept of himself, knowing that the thought of the **Infinite** is that of perfection, wholeness, and well-being. I announce this truth to myself until there is no longer anything in my thought that questions the truth of my statement about John Smith.

The **One Perfect Life** of the **Infinite** flows through John Smith now. It has always flowed through him. It is whole and complete. Nothing in the universe has the power to upset it or to obstruct it, for it is the resistless movement of **Omnipotence** in and through him.

His apparent illness is real only in a secondary sense. Perfection and wholeness are primary **Reality.** I look straight through the apparent reality to that which is primary. One constructive thought is more potent than ten thousand destructive thoughts. I speak my declaration of truth concerning John Smith with the quiet confidence that **now — at this very moment —** his illness is no more real than the horrors of a nightmare, and that he is awakening to his true state in which the false pictures of his nightmare disappear.

John Smith is **now** whole, complete, lacking nothing. He is expressing the **Divine** nature, through the unhindered working of the **Infinite Healing Presence** in him. It must be so, and it **is** so!

I now **release** my word to **deeper mind,** turning the entire responsibility for the manifestation over to it.

With this, the practitioner **releases** the healing process to the **Infinite Healing Presence,** synonymous with **Universal Mind,** and which works through **deeper mind,** the only agency that can change the thought into the thing, the only agency that possesses all the knowledge of the way to produce perfect cells in place of the former imperfect cells. He **releases** it with perfect confidence to **deeper mind,** where willingness to **obey** and the ability to do are the characteristics of this healing **mind** operating through **Law.**

THE ANALYTICAL, OR REASONING, METHOD

The Analytical Method is more extensive, but better suited to those of an analytical turn of mind. I use it more often, because I prefer to approach such things from a **reasoning** point of view, and to **analyze** and dissect the process of treatment. There is an added benefit in it because it breaks the treatment into seven steps; thus, when the results are not satisfactory, it furnishes an opportunity to determine at which step the treatment was not effective.

In the Analytical, or Reasoning, Method, the treatment is comparable to a golf swing, which appears to the uninitiated to be one continuous movement, but is really a great many steps perfectly coordinated. The golfer must set his feet at exact positions, grasp the club, and, without taking his eyes off the ball, bring the club back slowly, and on the down-swing gradually accelerate its rate; then, after he has hit the ball, still keep his eyes on the spot where the ball had been. There are many more components of a correct golf swing; these are given as examples.

When he is "off his game," a golfer can ask the instructor to play a round with him and watch him. If his trouble is a body sway, the professional will say, "I see where your trouble is. You're not keeping your body in line; you sway just a little as you make your stroke." When the golfer corrects this one step, his shots become good again. Yet, without breaking down the swing into its component parts, the instructor would have found it difficult to know just what the golfer was doing that was not correct.

It is for the same purpose that we have broken down treatment by the Analytical Method into seven steps. We call these steps the Seven "R's."

THE SEVEN "R'S"
FIRST "R" — RELAXATION

Physical relaxation

There must be both bodily and mental **relaxation.** Assume a position in which there is as little physical tension as possible. The posture doesn't matter so much — some treat standing, some sitting, some walking quietly, some lying down — but one must be physically **relaxed.**

Regarding position: When one falls asleep, as happens when the **surface mind** goes off the job, he tends to assume a recumbent position. This proves that one consciously has to use direction over the muscles to maintain a standing or a sitting position, but we do this so easily that we don't notice we are maintaining a certain muscular tension in any but the lying down position; therefore, the least tensed — or most **relaxed** — position is that of lying down. This means that all our thought, both **surface** and **deeper,** can go into the treatment.

Yet, unconsciously, sometimes the fingers will clench, or in some other way the muscles of the body will tense; so it is always

99

well to "shake oneself out" all over to be sure one has achieved complete physical **relaxation.**

Mental and emotional relaxation

More important, however, is **mental** and **emotional relaxation.** A tensed practitioner simply cannot get results, no matter how well he has learned the techniques of treatment. The student must remember that all of himself goes into his treatment. This means that no matter what words he uses to formulate the truth, a tenseness in his **inner** self will partially or completely nullify those words.

Words are secondary to the myriad streams of deeper thought that sweep in and swirl about a treatment. Since a person is the sum total of all he has ever experienced, if there are deeply hidden and, as yet, unresolved conflicts within the practitioner, these will affect his treatment to the degree of their intensity because all **mental** and **emotional** undercurrents enter into a treatment.

— imperfect persons can treat successfully

This does not mean that the practitioner must be near perfect in order to give an effective healing treatment. It does mean that if he carries a crippling memory of some past hurt, he must do something about it. Any experience that leads to self-pity must be healed. Any person who thinks that life has not treated him fairly, or who carries a grudge against someone who has wronged him, positively must resolve that problem if he is to be a good practitioner.

This might look as though it refers to getting straight with someone that we have wronged. But it applies equally to our feeling of being wronged. The net result of either experience is a feeling of separation. The practitioner must have a feeling of **oneness** with all. He can hold no hard feelings. It may not be possible or even necessary that he go in person to have matters straightened out. The chief necessity is that he straighten out his own feelings toward those who have wronged or hurt him.

— cleanse the inner life

Envy is another tensing emotion. The practitioner must be clean from all feelings of envy toward anyone more successful, more prosperous, more attractive, or healthier. It is quite understandable that we wish we were blessed as some others are blessed, and this is well; but the positive attitude toward this wishing is a quiet determination to emulate their success. The attainment of others can be turned into the spark that fires us to greater endeavor; thus it becomes a constructive stimulus. The very fact of inwardly rejoicing that others have received much blessing often is the key to our own blessing.

Envy is negative because it spells separation from others. By seeing their success as something distant from us, we unconsciously feel separated from them. Unless we rejoice with them, we are really believing that the greater heights attained by them are denied to us.

On the other hand, the desire to emulate is positive because it spells **unification**. It is the viewing of greater heights with which we may **unify** ourselves in consciousness, see ourselves experiencing them, and thereby set in motion the **Law** that will bring us to them. The very feeling that we are on our way, even though we have not yet arrived, is conducive to **relaxation** because it is free from any bitterness at our less satisfactory performance.

Jealousy, censoriousness, and any other hostile feelings must vanish also, for they are definitely separative feelings.

— the whole life goes into the treatment

It can readily be seen that to be a successful practitioner one must maintain a high standard of life. This really is the only satisfying kind of life, for it is the pathway to peace and to achievement of the goals that every one of us desires to reach whether we wish to study further and become professional practitioners or not. It means building into the character those elements of serenity, courage, optimism, and good will that make for an attractive personality, and that also lay the foundation for excellent health and prosperity.

While this sort of character makes for success in any profession, it is imperative in a spiritual practitioner. He who is sunk in gloom cannot treat others into a state of happiness. He who is burdened with debt does not easily treat others into prosperity. He who would save others from adverse circumstances must first save himself.

Yet he need not be completely free before he starts treating. Remembering that the outer manifestation is only the shadow of that which first was formed on the hidden side of his life, he achieves a **consciousness** of his freedom before his outward circumstances manifest it. The reality is the **thought**. If he has faced his difficulties and has achieved a reasonable mastery over them, he can begin to treat for others. But, I repeat, the first step in successful treating is **relaxation,** and by far the most important part of it is a **relaxed** mind.

SECOND "R" — RECOGNITION

The second step is Recognition. We must **recognize** that we are surrounded by an ocean of **Mind,** in which lie all the answers to all the problems of the world, a **Mind** that is characterized by

Omnipotence, Omniscience, and Omnipresence, and that is completely obedient, or responsive, to our thought.

OMNIPOTENCE — ALL POWER

We recognize that we are dealing with Omnipotence — all the Power in the universe. Thinking of God quantitatively, the average human thinks that if a certain amount of power is exercised at a certain point, there must be less left for other points. In the Science of Mind, we endeavor to see that at all times all of God is present at every point, and that no matter at how many points the healing streams are flowing, there is just as much flowing through our word for this person for whom we are treating as there was before, and just as much for our own needs as we can take.

All Omnipotence is present at every point. Each man can consider himself the recipient of everything the Father has or is without depriving anyone else.

Thus, when we treat, we call in, not some Power, but All-Power, and our neighbor does the same at the same time. This is the recognition that makes a powerful practitioner.

OMNISCIENCE — ALL KNOWLEDGE

There is not a problem in the universe to which Omniscience does not know the answer. Omniscience has brought into being everything that is. It has built every cell of the body, every successful life, for "without it was not anything made that was made." Man has problems; Omniscience has nothing but answers; it knows nothing of problems. Its knowledge is so far beyond anything that man has yet discovered that it knows nothing of "incurable" diseases. Man is proud of his scientific "discoveries"; yet Omniscience knew them all before the foundation of the world.

OMNIPRESENCE — EVERYWHERE PRESENT

Omnipresence means that the Infinite is equally present at all points in space; therefore, one can treat for a person living on the other side of the world just as easily as if he were in the same room. The practitioner does not project his thought at the person for whom he is treating; if he did, the treatment would become weaker in direct ratio to the distance.

We live in the surrounding ocean of Infinite Mind. The patient and the practitioner are both surrounded by it just as they are both surrounded by the physical atmosphere of the earth. That which is known at one point in that Mind is simultaneously known at every other point; therefore, that which the practitioner declares to be the truth about the patient is immediately known at the point in **Mind** where the patient is.

That is why distance between practitioner and patient is no barrier to effective treatment. Mrs. Bailes and I have treated for persons ten thousand miles distant, and the healing has taken place, sometimes simultaneously.

During a treatment, the practitioner substitutes his perfect thought about the patient for the patient's imperfect thought about himself, and **releases** his perfect thought into the **Infinite Mind,** which is everywhere present. This **Mind,** streaming through the patient and now carrying his picture of perfect health, proceeds to fabricate that perfect thought into form, which becomes the state of the patient.

The next lesson will bring this out even more clearly. We have covered in this lesson only the first two of the seven steps in the Analytical Method of treatment.

SPECIAL HELPS IN STUDY
AND PRACTICAL APPLICATION

These special helps have been carefully prepared to help you get the most out of this course.

Questions on the lesson

I advise that you first study the lesson carefully, then put it aside, write the answers to the questions, and, finally, **check your answers by the lesson.**

Keep the answers as a running commentary on the course **for your own benefit.** At its conclusion, you will find they have become a record of your own growth in consciousness.

1. What is a treatment?

2. What does the practitioner work with in a treatment?

3. When is a treatment completed?

4. In treating for another person, why do we use the third person instead of the second?

5. Comment on the relation between frequency of treatment and release.

6. What attitude should we take toward time in healing?

7. Explain the Realization Method of treatment.

8. How does the Analytical Method of treatment differ from the Realization Method?

9. How may one achieve the Relaxation Step in the Analytical Method?

10. Explain the Recognition Step, including its tremendous significance in healing.

Collateral reading suggestions

Frederick Bailes: "Help Answer Your Own Prayers"

Hidden Power for Human Problems, Ch. 12

Your Mind Can Heal You, Ch. V, pp. 99-106 (1941) pp. 86- 92 (1971)

Ervin Seale: The Great Prayer

Practical application

. . . thought-training

Examine your thought, and whatever you find in it that is keeping you from the best possible mental and emotional relaxation rid yourself of by using your powers of **selection** and **initiative.**

Whenever it comes to mind, select the opposite thought or a thought of **Omnipotence, Omniscience,** or **Omnipresence,** and begin making it a part of your thinking.

. . . writing suggestion

Write a treatment for yourself or someone else using the Realization Method.

. . . treatment for general good

This day I enter into a conscious acceptance of harmony.

I let go of all hurt feelings and self-pity even though I may have felt they have a legitimate basis.

I freely forgive myself for allowing myself to be hurt, and I generously forgive those whose words or actions gave rise to my inharmony.

I give of my love and my kindness this day, and I confidently expect the same from everyone I meet.

I let go of all anxiety concerning the past or the future.

I affirm this day that the entire universe backs me in my endeavors; that hidden currents of energy from **Infinite Mind** are now my inspiration; that everything in the universe is united in a benevolent conspiracy for my good.

And it **is** so.

Lesson 8

THE TECHNIQUE OF TREATMENT
(Continued)

THIRD "R" — RELATIONSHIP

The nature of the **Infinite**

— eternality of energy and **Substance**
— God as **Impersonal Principle**
— the **Personal** quality of God

Relationship of kind rather than of degree
— like unites with like

FOURTH "R" — REASONING

Why we reason
How we reason

FIFTH "R" — REALIZATION

Knowing is higher than feeling

SIXTH "R" — RELEASE

Responsibility is on **Mind,** not on us

SEVENTH "R" — REJOICING

**SUMMARY OF THE SEVEN "R'S"
OF THE ANALYTICAL METHOD**

PRACTICAL POINTS IN TREATMENT

We use the third person
We do not petition
We speak with authority

CULTIVATE EXPECTANCY OF RESULTS

107

EIGHTH LESSON
GOALS

To understand the Seven "R's"
   of the Analytical, or Reasoning,
   Method of treatment

To make definite progress
   in establishing a closer
   relationship with the **Infinite**

"THIRD "R" — RELATIONSHIP

The third "R" in the Analytical Method of treatment is Relationship. Having brought oneself into the properly **relaxed** state physically and mentally, and having come into a **recognition** of the **Power** with which he works, the practitioner might still feel that he is not a part of this **Power.** He might agree that it exists as part of the nature of the **Infinite,** but that he himself, being a struggling, faulty human being, is something apart and separate from it. It is important, therefore, that he comes into a clear understanding of his **relationship** to this **Power.** To acquire this understanding, it is necessary to go into the varied interpretations of the nature of God.

I as your teacher am reluctant to do this, for I know that each of us has his own personal set of beliefs about God and the spiritual world. I have no desire to interfere with the cherished beliefs of any of my students, but I believe that a clear-eyed approach to the puzzling question of the unseen forces of the universe can never interfere with the real fundamentals of any religious faith.

Moreover, the approach that we take in these lessons seems not to be incompatible with the beliefs of any religious group. The thousands upon thousands of students who have taken my courses have come from virtually every religious faith known to man. These students have often told me that they have found nothing in this approach that would interfere with their particular religious faith. On the contrary, many of them have said that they never really understood the hidden forces of the universe in creation until they found our approach.

This approach does not violate the processes of reason, and it leads the student into a sense of intimate **relationship** with the **Creator.** This latter I take to be the end and purpose of any true religion.

In addition, our approach sets up the sort of **relationship** with the **Infinite** that works out in a very practical way in the increasing of all those blessings and virtues that bring man into a state that is usually called "happiness." It is a practical approach to the entire matter of healing the ills of humanity.

The nature of the Infinite

Throughout the ages theologians have manfully struggled with the concept of the nature of God. They have done their best, but their efforts have ranged all the way from the crude concepts of primitive man, through the stiff dogmas of the Dark and Middle Ages, to the more enlightened concepts of modern man. Yet, in this twentieth century, all three of these types of thinking prevail in various religious circles, and, unfortunately, some men who

109

secretly think differently are compelled to preach archaic beliefs or lose their pulpits and their livelihood.

Perhaps George Bernard Shaw spoke the truth when he said there is only one religion in the entire world but at least a hundred versions of it.

Probably the key to the question lies in one's view of the **Personality** of God. Is God **Personality** or **Impersonal Principle?** We believe that He is a combination of both.

— eternality of energy and Substance

Lesson 4 showed the three phases of the **Trinity** to be **Spirit, Mind,** and **Body.** No one of the three created the others, for all three were present from the beginning, the only exception being that **Body** was not yet formed; it was present then only as the **Primary Unformed Substance** of the universe.

The principles of the conservation of matter and the conservation of energy state, in effect, that matter and energy are equally indestructible and, therefore, are eternal in that their sum total is never increased nor diminished, but merely changed from one form into another. A piece of paper burns up, yet does not go out of existence except in its papery form. It has changed its form into ash and gases; yet none of it has been rendered non-existent. Scientists tell us there is always precisely the same amount.

A meteorite passing through the earth's atmosphere has motion, which is converted into heat; then the heat is converted into light; but the quantity is never diminished even in the meteorite burned up to what we call "nothing."

The term "God" is difficult to define, for everything seen and unseen is some part of this **Three-Phased Intelligence** that we call "God." Our bodies are the extension of the **Unformed Substance,** which is the **Body** of God. Our **minds** are the extension of God as **Mind.** Our **spirit** is the extension of God as **Spirit.** Man is linked at every point to the **Three-Sided Infinite.** Man expresses very imperfectly in the relative what God is in the **Perfect Absolute.**

Our **relationship,** therefore, is both **personal** and **impersonal.**

— God as Impersonal Principle

The atmosphere, which is part of the **Body** of God, presses **impersonally** and equally upon each of the more than three and a half billions of earth's inhabitants. **Life,** that greatest of all mysteries, flows **impersonally** through us all. Contrary to the opinion of many, a prosperous material supply flows **impersonally** throughout the universe, and is drawn toward the person whose consciousness attracts it. The universe is **impersonal** toward its inhabitants in that the sunlight and the rain fall upon the just and the unjust; the earth will respond to anyone's cultivation; the seas will float anyone's boat; gravitation pulls all men equally.

In like manner, the stream of consciousness will quite **impersonally** make one person well and another ill according to the quality of their thought. Thought flows by **Law** just as electricity does, and will destroy one or build him up, just as electricity will make toast for us or electrocute us, **depending upon whether we adjust to, or violate, the law of its action.**

From this point of view, there is a phase of God that is entirely **Impersonal,** operating equally everywhere in this **impersonal** manner.

When man understands this, he will no longer rail against God for the damage done by tornado, earthquake, and hurricane, which are the result of natural law, and which have an ultimate stabilizing effect in the structure and operation of the physical universe. A reasoning man adjusts to meteorological violence either by not settling in certain areas, or by making provision for it. God does not force him to live there any more than He forces him to build his house on a sand dune.

In like manner, the truly well-instructed person will never give up his faith in God at the death of a loved one. He will never say, "I prayed and prayed to what I thought was a loving Father. I promised to dedicate my whole life to Him if He would save my loved one, but He turned His back on me in my hour of greatest need."

If God would set aside the **impersonal** laws of the universe to save me from being injured by those laws, the whole universe would collapse in ruin and debris. It is our business as individuals to discover the laws that govern the universe and to adjust our thinking to them.

So much for the **Impersonal** side of the nature of God as evidenced in the vast field of physical and mental **Law.**

— the Personal quality of God

But man introduces the **Personal** element when he begins to recognize or to seek union with the **Infinite.**

Rufus Jones has used an appropriate term — the "Double Search." He reasons that man has an instinct for God that impels him ever to seek to find his way back into union with the **Infinite.** But he says that man's search is only the answering search; the Original Search is that of the **Infinite** for union with man, and man's search is his unconscious response to God's nudging of him.

Man's predecessors came from that long line of physical organisms dating back to the first living cell. Each of those predecessors was of a lower order than man; therefore, they were incapable of originating a spiritual impulse; so his spiritual out-

111

reaching could not have come from his physical nature. This spiritual hunger, then, must be the outreaching of God for man, and man's desire for union with the **Infinite** must be his intuitive response to this, hence the term "Double Search."

We mentioned before the difficulty of defining God or describing His nature with any detailed accuracy, but it is at the point of man's intuitive response to the Original Search that God becomes **Personal**. There must be some larger sense in which God is **Personal,** but it is far beyond the comprehension of finite man who invariably connects personality with form or with the attributes that we associate with our human personality, as the Greeks did with their Olympian gods.

The way the **Law of Creativeness** responds to man's thought makes it seem humanly personal so that it is, at the same time, both **Personal** and **Impersonal.** More than this it is not necessary to say at this time.

I am a little suspicious of the person who dogmatically states that his concept of God is the correct one. God is the Great Mystery. Our views are based upon what we can see of His operations throughout the universe.

Relationship of kind rather than of degree

The **relationship,** then, is that of a union of kind rather than of degree.

— like unites with like

That which is in harmony tends to unify with that with which it is in harmony. It follows, then, that as our thought clears itself of earthiness, it moves into closer harmony with that of the **Infinite,** and a close working bond is established.

For example, he whose heart is filled with hate and prejudice cannot establish the right **relationship** with **Creative Law,** which springs from a **Love Source.** He who is filled with fear is not in unison with that which has never known fear.

We do not have to be perfect in our mental freedom, but we must be willing and ready to drop the ugly, deforming thought-patterns if we are to move into this relationship that precedes the healing of ourselves and others. Man has a long, long way to go in his search for perfection. He should be grateful that he can reproduce the nature of God to the extent of using the **Creative Process** even in spite of his human weaknesses.

So long as we are willing to let go those destructive moods, we are establishing the proper **relationship** with the **Infinite.** Thus we are to that extent merged with His thought, which can then flow through our thought-patterns with all its healing knowledge, for, in the final analysis, it is always the **Infinite Healing Presence** that heals.

It has been said, "In Him we live and move and have our being." This is the original part of the Double Search; the responsive part is that in which **we** let **Him** "live, move, and have His being" in us. We in Him, He in us. "I am in the Father and He in me."

It is as though we should toss a biscuit into the ocean. It would be in the ocean, but, as it stayed there, the ocean would gradually seep through it and be **in it.**

The good practitioner — and remember that by "practitioner" we mean anyone who practices the Science of Mind — is a God-saturated person, forever drawing upon all the abilities of that which saturates him, and forever yielding to that which saturates. His power lies not in himself, but in that with which he is in **relationship.** He whose **relationship** is closer with the negative will manifest the negative. He whose closer harmonies are with that which is "true, honest, just, pure, lovely, and of good report" will manifest these.

FOURTH "R" — REASONING

The fourth "R" is Reasoning. In the Analytical Method, this is used more than in the Realization Method; yet even in the latter there is a lightninglike or instantaneous **reasoning.**

Why we reason

Reasoning is for the purpose of dissolving the practitioner's doubts. We must remember that the treatment begins and ends within the mind of the practitioner, in that he works upon his own belief rather than on that of the patient. Thus we shall see the value of **reasoning.**

Let us suppose we are going to give treatment for a person with an illness. We start to treat by immediately declaring his perfection, but at once an image of his disability comes before us. Perhaps the doctor has told him that his condition is incurable, and this prognosis comes before us. The memory of our own faults or any one of a hundred different forms of negative thinking rises to make us waiver. To dispel these doubts and ugly pictures, we resort to **reasoning** as a salesman deals with the objections of the man he is trying to sell.

How we reason

We may begin by calling up memories of someone else who had this or another equally "incurable" condition, and we argue with ourselves that the **Infinite Healing Presence** was well able to deal with it, because the sufferer was completely healed. At first, we shall need to think of healings we have heard of or read about, but soon we ourselves shall have treated persons back into health. Then we can call upon our own experience.

Or we may begin to **reason** about the undefeatable **Power** of the **Omnipotent Infinite** as shown in and through nature. We think of the tremendous force that holds a myriad suns in place, moving them effortlessly through space, always on time to the split second. Then we argue with ourselves that this apparently big problem that confronts us is infinitesimal to such a **Power.**

We remember that we treat the thought rather than the physical condition. We **reason** that the condition is entirely a thing of thought, and that constructive thought is ten thousand times more powerful than destructive thought; therefore, this constructive thought of ours, being brought into line with the **Infinite,** is in line with the **Infinite Will,** and has **Power** over the destructive pattern. We remember that as the thought alters, there will be a corresponding change in the physical.

Thus we **reason** our way to the point where all our inner objections are answered, and all inner doubts are removed.

FIFTH "R" — REALIZATION

The fifth "R" is Realization. When there is nothing any longer in our own thinking that denies the truth of these statements that we are making concerning this person's perfection, we arrive at the **realization** of healing. Everything within us in our deepest self now nods assent to the declarations we are quietly making regarding the **Infinite Perfection** that is now spreading in and throughout his whole thought structure and flowing from this into the cells of his body, his business, his home, and all his other affairs. At this stage, we **realize** that the healing is now launched and on its way.

At this stage, we **realize** also that we are not speaking our word into a void, but that we are impressing it upon the receptive and obedient **Mind** of the **Infinite.** We **realize** that there is not the slightest reason why our word should not have power and not the least occasion for doubt and, furthermore, not any reluctance upon the part of the **Infinite** to flow into form in accordance with this perfect picture we are presenting to it. And we are so convinced of the truth of our conviction that any fear of failure would be unthinkable.

Knowing is higher than feeling

In this stage, there may be a sense of great uplift, or there may be none. Remember, our feelings lie in the field of emotions, which might or might not back up our conviction; therefore, do not feel that the treatment has not been a good one if the rising tide of emotion is absent. It is well when we "feel" the truth we are declaring, but it is infinitely better when we **know** the truth we are declaring. **Knowing** is always higher than feeling, and our

114

demonstrations are made upon what we **know,** rather than upon what we feel.

On the other hand, times will come when the practitioner is lifted to a very lofty altitude, when it seems as if the earth recedes and the spiritual world becomes very real. Doubts, uncertainties, and self-condemnation are all passed away, and one enters into a sense of union with the **Infinite** that is so real he feels there never were any problems and never will be any. Don't seek this, but if it comes, surrender yourself to it, for it is a high point of **realization.**

SIXTH "R" — RELEASE

The sixth "R" is Release. When one comes to the place where his doubts have been replaced by a deep conviction of the truth he is declaring, he quickly moves on to the next stage — **release.** Keeping in mind that it is not we who produce the results, we quickly **release** our perfectly formed picture of our patient to the **Infinite Mind,** which is always entirely receptive to our thought. Our responsibility is to present the perfect picture of the patient, then **release** it to **Mind.**

The **Creative Mind** is the only agency in the universe that can transform thoughts into things; in fact, this is what it is doing every moment of the time. It has turned our patient's destructive thought into illness. It will now turn our constructive thought into health as it flows through him.

We shall think of this **Infinite Mind** as a river into which the thoughts of the race are constantly falling. Its business is constantly to fabricate these thoughts into form. This river flows equally through all men, and is called "their" minds as it passes through their brains. Healing others at any distance is possible because **Infinite Mind** receives our perfect thought and carries it through that one for whom we are treating.

Thus it is not a question of how much mental force the practitioner can generate to force his mental pattern over a great distance to someone else; the secret of healing lies in the completeness with which one **releases** his thought and word to this river of **Mind.**

Responsibility is on Mind, not on us

Having **released** it, we drop all responsibility for making our word come to pass. That responsibility belongs to **Mind.** Ours is only to make sure that we **release** as perfect a picture to that **Mind** as is possible. We don't try to push it or help in any way except by not allowing discordant or doubtful thoughts to enter our mind in regard to the one for whom we treated. "The Father that dwelleth in me, He doeth the works." "I know whom I have believed and am persuaded that He is able to keep that which I have committed unto Him against that day [of manifestation]."

To repeat what we said in the last lesson: It is sufficient to treat two or three times daily for the person. If you find yourself wanting to treat too often, you have not **released** the treatment completely. Whenever the thought of the patient enters your mind between treatments, just say, "I'm glad I've turned it over to **Infinite Mind**," and **release** it again.

Releasing is a highly important part of treatment. Unfortunately, some beginners, as well as some experienced students, have difficulty in learning to **release** completely. Try to step out from under the sense of responsibility. Let your thought about the person himself go completely into the care of the **Infinite.** We could not think steadily all day of a person for whom we treat, but we can turn our treatment over to the **Infinite,** which easily carries our thought about all our patients. It never forgets. It never grows weary. **Release! Release! Release!**

SEVENTH "R" — REJOICING

The seventh "R" is Rejoicing. One never is happy over good things that do not come to pass. He **rejoices** at completion and accomplishment. We therefore **give thanks** as soon as we have released our word to the **Infinite.** This is "giving substance to things hoped for, evidence to things not seen."

Rejoicing and **giving thanks** are not for the purpose of influencing the **Infinite.** They are for their effect upon the practitioner. If an unreliable person promises to give us something at a later date, and especially if his promises were never kept in the past, we might politely thank him, but inwardly there would be no rejoicing because we would not believe he would fulfill his promise.

But if a loved one who always keeps his word promises us something in the future, we immediately begin to **rejoice** in it even before we have it in our hands because we actually believe — in fact, we know — that he will give it. Our belief in the **Infinite Responsiveness** leads us to **give thanks** at once, and our **giving thanks** helps confirm our confidence in it.

These are the seven component parts of the treatment.

SUMMARY OF THE SEVEN "R'S" OF THE ANALYTICAL METHOD

1. RELAXATION

We take a physically relaxed position.

We relax mentally by cleansing our thought-life and achieving at least a reasonable mastery over personal problems.

2. RECOGNITION

We recognize that we are surrounded by an **Infinite Ocean of Mind** that receives the imprint of our word; that what is known at one point is known at all points; and that it responds instantly and automatically.

3. **RELATIONSHIP**

We are permeated by this **Infinite Mind** as a biscuit in the ocean would be permeated by the ocean.

4. **REASONING**

We reason away doubts.

5. **REALIZATION**

We **know** this is the truth about us or about the person.

6. **RELEASE**

We release this truth to the **Infinite Ocean of Mind.**

7. **REJOICING**

We give thanks because we know we shall receive.

PRACTICAL POINTS IN TREATMENT

We use the third person

As we said in the preceding lesson, a treatment for another is always carried on in the third person, never in the second. We never say, "John Smith, you are well"; instead we say "John Smith is well." We talk about the patient, not to him. What we say to him in a conversation is not a treatment. What we say about him when he is not with us is the treatment.

We do not petition

We offer no petition in the treatment. We do not say, "Please grant healing to him." Instead, we make declarations and assertions about him: that he is already perfect in the eyes of the **Infinite;** that he is free from false beliefe; that his body and his whole outer affairs are now manifesting his changed belief. We make the statement, "Perfect God, perfect man (woman), perfect structure, perfect function. This is the truth about him at this very moment — **now.**"

We speak with authority

We go further. "Thou shalt decree a thing, and it shall be established unto thee." We inject a note of **authority** into our treatment so that instead of begging or hoping that something will happen, we decree that it shall happen. This does not mean that we are "bossing" God; it means that we recognize the **Creative Law** as being completely obedient to our word. We do not "boss" the filling station attendant, but we do order ten gallons of gasoline, and we fully expect him to give it to us. We would be amazed if he should tell us he doesn't think gasoline is good for us; therefore, he must refuse to give it to us. We decree gasoline for us; he obeys our decree.

117

CULTIVATE EXPECTANCY OF RESULTS

In the beginning, some students are astounded when the **Law** works for them. They should be astounded when it seems not to work for them. Naturally, there is rejoicing when we see our word coming into form, but soon this is replaced by a more settled expectancy as we see more and more manifestations coming forth in response to our treatment.

If you have not already begun to treat for someone else, I suggest you begin now. You will be helping those you treat for, and you will be growing in consciousness as you do.

When a person is physically and mentally able to take part in helping himself, I believe he should do so. There are, however, situations in which it is not possible; for example, the mentally ill, people too physically ill to be told, small children, and people not acquainted with this way of thought. The student who has grasped these lessons on technique will not have to be reminded that in treating for others we never treat that they do some particular thing, but that they **be** the persons they are intended to be.

Small children usually reflect the thought-patterns of their parents, nurses, and others in their environment; therefore, in treating for a child, we should treat for these other persons as well as for the child himself.

"Each victory will help you some other to win."

SPECIAL HELPS IN STUDY
AND PRACTICAL APPLICATION

These special helps have been carefully prepared to help you get the most out of this course.

Questions on the lesson

I advise that you first study the lesson carefully, then put it aside, write the answers to the questions, and, finally, **check your answers by the lesson.**

Keep the answers as a running commentary on the course **for your own benefit.** At its conclusion, you will find they have become a record of your own growth in consciousness.

1. What is meant by "God as **Impersonal Principle**"?

2. What is meant by "the **Personal** quality of God"?

3. Why do we say that man's Relationship to God is of kind rather than degree?

4. Explain the Reasoning Step of treatment.

5. Why is the Realization Step the high point of treatment?

6. Why is the Release Step so important?

7. What is the purpose of the Rejoicing Step?

8. What is the difference between talking with a patient and giving treatment for him?

9. Instead of petitioning in a treatment, what do we do?

10. Why can we speak with authority?

Collateral reading suggestions

Frederick Bailes: Hidden Power for Human Problems,
        Ch. 12

        Your Mind Can Heal You, Ch. V,
          pp. 106-118 (1941)
          pp. 92-102 (1971)

Basil King: The Conquest of Fear

Practical application

. . . thought-training

In order to bring yourself into a closer relationship with the **Infinite,** test your thought by Phil. 4:8.

Is it true, honest, just, pure, lovely, and of good report?

. . . writing suggestion

Write a treatment for yourself or someone else using the Analytical, or Reasoning, Method, and giving careful attention to the Seven ''R's.''

. . . a treatment for general good

I understand that I am one with all the constructive forces of the universe, and that all the harmonious currents of **Life** are drawn to me and operate through me.

I have established a right relation to **Infinite Mind.**

I am surrounded by perfect understanding this day as I make contacts with other persons.

All my domestic, social, and occupational relationships are marked by **Infinite Harmony.**

I have mentally established a right relation to others.

My body reflects this understanding.

Each tiny pinpoint experiences harmony within itself and with the surrounding cells.

All the parts harmoniously co-operate with one another to the end that health is my experience.

Health, happiness, a sense of extreme well-being, come from my understanding of my relation to the constructive forces of the universe.

And it **is** so.

Lesson 9

TREATMENT FOR SPECIFIC CONDITIONS

STOMACH ULCERS

False belief in irritation

— nothing can irritate us without our consent

Sample treatment for irritation

PRACTICAL POINTS IN TREATMENT

Name the person

Treat the belief

— buried racial beliefs — the race mind

Recognize that man is the **Infinite** bounded by form

Speak with authority

SUPPLY

Spiritual basis for supply

— through the apparent to the real

Treating for supply

Sample treatment for supply

— an analysis of the sample treatment for supply

COLDS

HEALING IS OF THE WHOLE PERSON

NINTH LESSON
GOALS

To understand the sample treatments
    for specific conditions

To make definite progress
    in working out your own treatments
    for specific conditions

We shall now devote three lessons to the ways of treating for various kinds of difficulties if and when they appear. Sample treatments will be given so the student will have them as guides to work out his own individual treatments for particular conditions of diverse nature.

The student must never forget that we treat the **thought** rather than the condition. This is because the condition is only the **thought** in form. Conditions are only effects; **thoughts** are the causes. Correct the causes and the effects correct themselves. We resolve the condition back into **thought;** then we dissolve the **thought** through treatment.

STOMACH ULCERS

Suppose we start with a physical condition such as stomach ulcers. There is nothing more physical in its manifestations than this ailment, and nothing more mental in its cause. One could persistently treat for the ulcers themselves to heal, and see no result; but when one treats for the underlying irritation in the **thought,** the ulcers heal.

False belief of irritation

Ulcers come in that person who has the false belief that something or someone outside of himself has the power to irritate him. The source of his irritation might be members of his family, those with or for whom he works, an environment with which he is not in agreement, the pressure of overwork, financial worries, or any one of a number of external experiences.

— nothing can irritate us without our consent

Experiences in themselves have no power to irritate us. It is our **reactions** to them that irritate. One person may say, "Green and red irritate and enrage me." The other says, "I simply adore red and green." Another says, "That Mrs. Smith's shrill cackle drives me wild." Her neighbor says, "I love to hear Mrs. Smith's merry laugh." Now, if there were some irritating quality **in** the colors or the laugh, it would irritate all equally; therefore, the irritation arises **within** the person and is his irritated **reaction** to something that is neutral.

The person who understands the Science of Mind knows that nothing in the universe has the inherent power to irritate him without his consent. He therefore **withholds his consent.** He **chooses** to hold quiet and steady in the presence of what others allow to irritate them, and he thus remains free from irritation. He who does not understand this is allowing himself to be irritated hourly.

We have said that while man thinks with every cell of his body, the cell has no individual intelligence, no power of independent thought; it must take on the thought-pattern of the person of whom it is a part. The waves of thought from the brain, carried over the network of fine threads called the nervous system, are momentarily sweeping the entire body; therefore, the cell has to think what the brain thinks, and the brain has to think what the person using it thinks.

Those successive waves of irritated thought flashing through-out the body begin to impart their irritating nature to the cells through which they pass. Certain organs and tissues seem to be more susceptible to irritation than others; therefore, the person finds an irritation of the skin or perhaps of a mucous membrane starting to bother him. Sinus trouble that has not been affected by change of climate has often been healed by healing the belief in irritation, as have all the various body conditions that arise from this false belief.

Heal the thought, and the body will heal itself.

Sample treatment for irritation

A treatment for this condition might be carried on along the following lines. The student may alter it or add to it to suit his own consciousness and the conditions involved.

I know that John Smith, of 1111 Blank Road, Townville, is an extension of **Infinite Mind;** therefore, what is true of it must be true of him.

Nothing in the universe has the power to irritate or disturb the **Infinite,** for it rests always in a state of perfect peace.

John Smith's false belief in the cause of his irritation has produced a bodily irritation. I now speak my perfect word, declaring that nothing in the universe has the power to irritate him, and that he knows this truth to be operating around and within him at this moment.

This new belief makes him quiet and serene in the presence of the most disturbing situations. He is held steady and tranquil by the action of **Spirit** deep within him. Peace is an everpresent reality to him.

New brain waves are sweeping over his body. The cells love this new-found peace; they rapidly build themselves according to the **Perfect Pattern.** The **Infinite Healing Presence** fills each cell with so much of itself that there is no room for anything else.

I release this word about John Smith, giving thanks for its perfect manifestation before I see it in form. My word decrees it into form; therefore, it must be so, and it **is** so.

PRACTICAL POINTS IN TREATMENT
Name the person

We have said that a treatment is a very definite thing for a definite purpose. We therefore give the name and address of the person for whom we are treating. If for some reason we do not know the address, the name will be specific enough for our purpose.

Treat the belief

It will be noticed in the sample treatment that we make little reference to the body. We lightly touch it in passing to indicate the specific condition for which we are treating, but we do not overstress it. Sometimes we use the words, "And I know that every cell of his body knows this truth that I speak, and is being remolded according to it." In one sense, there is nothing to heal; the illness lies in the false **belief.**

— buried racial beliefs — the race mind

The human race is only in its infancy. The connection between man's **thought** and his illnesses has only recently been accepted. If man had advanced to the stage where there was a universal **dis**belief in illness, there would be none of it for him to experience. Neither would there be any of the other miserable conditions under which mankind labors.

But mankind has not yet reached that stage, and so we in the Science of Mind have to use whatever method that we, as individuals, can use to separate ourselves from the false racial **beliefs,** and establish a personal **belief** of the unreality, or impermanence, of any experience that limits man's freedom. This personal **belief** is, at present, widely at variance with commonly accepted **beliefs;** therefore, it is not always easy to free ourselves from the drag of the race-thought.

This should not discourage us, nor should we be disheartened because the race is only starting to climb into spiritual realms. On the contrary, we should be very happy because it has made so much progress in so short a time. One encouraging feature is that the moment our personal **belief** can be lifted even a little higher, our outer manifestation will automatically rise that much higher. Even if we cannot rise into perfection immediately, we can at least grow in that direction, and there will be enough encouraging demonstrations to keep us moving upward.

Spiritual treatment is growing in use each year. It has been estimated that more than twenty million persons in the United States are using it today, and the number is growing. In twenty-five years, probably a hundred million will be using it throughout the world, and the race thought will be correspondingly more positive.

Recognize that man is the Infinite bounded by form

It is important that we see clearly that man is an **extension of the Infinite** as the inlet is of the ocean. This is to establish a basis of **oneness** upon which we can base our expectation of healing.

The inner world is the world of **Reality;** the outer world is that of the shadow thrown by the inner. There is no doubt but that a pain is real to our senses, or that a broken bone is broken, but the **Infinite** never experiences pain or fracture; therefore, our healing comes to the degree that we can establish our sense of **oneness of quality** with the **Infinite,** remembering that the **Infinite** is **Reality;** the body is shadow.

We repeat that a drop of sea water differs from the ocean only in size. Each drop chemically analyzes the same as the ocean. As far as water is concerned, the inlet is the ocean, the only difference being that it is "boundarized" into smaller form by shores that are easily seen.

Man is the **Infinite bounded by form.** This we must remember as we treat for ourselves and others, for it is the key to mental and spiritual healing. Man has the seeds of perfection in him, for he originates from a perfect **Source.** His spiritual center is perfect. His healing springs from this spiritual, perfect center.

Speak with authority

A treatment differs from the ordinary concept of prayer in that we do not abase ourselves, calling ourselves sinners and worms of the dust. We stand upon our inherent dignity as **extensions of the Infinite.** We speak with **authority** because we know that we reproduce the **Creative Cycle** that brought the world into being, and that, because of our unique **relationship** to God, our word could be as powerful as that of God if we could shake ourselves free of the race thought and actually believe, with all our hearts, that this **is** so.

We do not merely wish or hope for something to happen. We speak our word, **knowing** it will happen. In treatment, there is a decisiveness that is lacking in the older-style prayers, which frequently wobbled, because the person praying was never sure that what he was asking for was according to the will of God.

We have been seeing, during this course of lessons, that the will of God is anything that enlarges us or our happiness without hurting someone else. It is our duty to determine the integrity of our prayer (treatment) from this point of view. Then, having done this, we can treat with the completest assurance that there is nothing in the universe that wishes us not to have what we speak our word for.

SUPPLY

Suppose the problem is one of supply. The person has a false belief of stringency. We do not treat that money will pour into the life of this person even though that is what he wants, and we want him to have it. In an earlier lesson, we said that in the Sermon on the Mount, Jesus was dealing with deep, underlying beliefs. When he came to the subject of supply, he admitted that the people's desire for food and clothing was legitimate, but he tried to show them that if they would seek the **Giver,** the gifts would naturally follow.

Spiritual basis for supply

He talked of spiritually conceived **Supply** while their minds were on money. He talked of an **Inner Life** hidden within the lilies of the field which clothed the flowers with an outer beauty, but they were thinking of garments to cover their bodies. He talked of an endless store of **Supply** that had always been present there to keep the sparrows alive, but they were thinking of loaves of bread. In effect, he said, "For the time being, forget those things of sense, and seek the **Inner Kingdom** of God. Unite your consciousness with that of the **Giver,** who has never known lack; then, as a matter of course, these secondary things will all be added to you."

The man who sees loaves of bread and overcoats only, or sees them as the chief end of life, will have to scratch daily for another loaf and another coat. But he who drives past the loaf to the underlying **Principle** of an unfailing **Supply** will quietly know that there will be another loaf tomorrow. In fact, he can produce such a broad abundance that he never thinks of individual loaves. Though this distinction might not seem significant, it is one of the most important we can make for the following reasons:

The **Healing Principle** is far wider than health, which is only one of its manifestations. The **Principle** of **Supply** is far more extensive than money or food, which are only two of the manifestations. The **Principle** of **Harmony** is universal, rather than just individual, peace of mind; the latter is merely one of its manifestations. Underlying all things, we must find the **Principle** of that thing; then we can apply that **Principle** to a thousand particulars.

The **Kingdom** of God, so often mentioned by Jesus and the ancient seers, is the **consciousness** of the **oneness** of God and man, and God's pouring into man all of His abundance.

This **Kingdom** is sought by breaking free from the mass view, constantly lifting our thought to its highest levels, and seeing God as never reluctant to grant our desires, but rather ever seeking to express a more abundant life through us. It is the putting away of that which is petty, cruel, and censorious toward others, see-

127

ing them as also seeking the path to happiness even when they hurt us, forgiving them because "they know not what they do," helping them where we can, but never allowing ourselves to be bound by the quality of their thought.

— through the apparent to the real

It means the cultivating of our ability to pierce the veil of the material with all its seeming reality, and to penetrate to the **inner,** hidden world of true **Reality,** where all things have their origin, and whence all things emerge into the seen world. It means absorption in the contemplation of **Omniscience, Omnipotence,** and **Omnipresence,** with all their underlying **Principles,** and knowing that therein lies the true world of **causation.** It means concentrating on **causes** rather than effects, knowing that effects will assuredly come once the proper **causes** are set in motion. It is a movement from the **inner** side of life working itself toward the outer.

It is a reversal of the thinking of the majority and it produces striking results.

This is why we constantly stress the fact that we treat the **thought** rather than the condition. The true healing is the healing of the **thought;** the outward healing is the healed **thought** shadowed forth in this, our less real world of the outer. This is as Plato taught: that the real world is the **inner** world; the outer world is the shadow thrown by the real world within.

Treating for supply

In treating for prosperity, therefore, we do not treat for the ten-dollar bill; we get down to the unfailing **Principle** of **Supply.**

To return to our method: Again we start with the fact that man is in the small what God is in the large. We cannot conceive of the **Infinite** as ever being "short" of anything. Man believes he is short of things because he cannot or does not see the **Infinite Supply.** We correct or counteract his false belief.

We stress the obvious fact that **Supply** has been constant from his birth although the channels through which it has come have been many and varied. Starting with the infant's milk, he has had three meals a day until now, and he has been clothed and housed. That **Supply** has come through temporary channels such as his mother, his father, odd jobs in boyhood, steady jobs in manhood. In the latter case, some of the companies from which he drew his **Supply** may have gone out of business, or he may, voluntarily, have left their employ. But no matter for what reason, those channels were temporary.

The only changeless thing in this man's whole picture has been **Supply.** He may have thought that the company was supplying him because it gave him a pay check, but it was only the temporary channel through which this never-ceasing **Supply** was finding its way to him. Since it has been continuous in the past, he can logically expect it to be continuous in the future.

There has been no stoppage of **Supply** for the **Infinite;** there has been no stoppage for him. There will be no stoppage for the **Infinite;** there will be none for him. "Shall not your Father clothe you, O ye of little faith?"

Here is the crux: Man's **Supply** never fails from the other side, but, because of his little faith, he pinches it into a tiny trickle. He has developed false beliefs in obstruction and delay, and in the difficulty of **Infinite Mind's** turning invisible **Supply** into visible substance. It is no more difficult for **Mind** to make gold than to make sand or grass, but our **belief** makes it difficult.

Sample treatment for supply

I know that John Smith, of 1111 Blank Road, Townville, is in the small what the **Infinite** is in the large. He is forever in touch with an **Infinite Supply,** of which there can never be any shortage or depletion.

His false belief has turned his mind toward channels instead of toward the **Reservoir.** He has allowed his fears to clog up his channels. He has had his mind on the particular rather than on the general, on channels rather than on the fact that **Supply** is never failing, on things rather than on **Principles.**

In this moment, I turn away from his financial needs, debts, obligations, where his thought has so long lingered. I turn to the great, unchanging **Principle** of **Supply.** I seek for him the inner **Kingdom** of God. I see him united with a never-ceasing flow of good, which takes the form of that which he needs in his outer affairs.

I speak my word, knowing that his consciousness is now wide open to the **Resources** of the **Infinite,** and that there is nothing in his belief that hinders their flow through him. Opportunities are now presenting themselves to him, doors are opening to him as his consciousness awakens, people are seeing his true worth, and he is amply and adequately compensated for whatever effort he puts forth.

Supply flows through his consciousness easily, freely, copiously, continuously, effortlessly, and manifests itself in his outer affairs.

I release this word to that **Infinite Servant** that pours **Supply** this day into more than three and a half billion earth dwellers, as well as feeding the countless trillions of lower forms of life from its inexhaustible **Resources.** It controls a million worlds in space, easily and effortlessly. John Smith's fullest, most copious supply is infinitesimal to it.

I therefore give thanks for it even before John Smith and I see it in form, because it **is** so.

— an analysis of the sample treatment for supply

The student will notice that we have used the idea of John Smith's **true worth** and **value** being recognized. Very often the person in need thinks only of what he wants instead of what he has to **give.** No one helps us out of our poverty just because he likes to do so. Our treatment for John is partially a treatment of prospective employers and customers, who will see the worth of John's goods or his services and want to avail themselves of them.

The treatment also helps correct John's faulty view, turning it from wanting to **giving.** Every contract must be equally valuable to the two parties. It is not enough to take pity on John and give him a job. He must have something that is valuable to that employer, or the bargain is unfair. Moreover, John must himself be conscious of his **true worth** if others are to come into that same consciousness.

John's trouble is not lack, but a belief in his worthlessness. He may strenuously deny this, saying that he is a better worker than nine tenths of those employed; but somewhere in his **deeper mind** there is always some sense of insufficiency, either unrecognized or unadmitted, which keeps him from richly paid employment. The student must treat this false belief, or John will lose the next job he gets or the next money he saves.

Few uninstructed persons know the extreme complexity of their **deeper minds,** and seldom dream of the real **causes** of their difficulties. The student must treat for them accordingly.

COLDS

In treating for the person with a cold or similar ailments, it is necessary to know that the wet feet or the draught is only the exciting cause of the trouble. The underlying, predisposing cause is confusion, usually accompanied by strong feelings of inner rage and frustration. This is supported by thousands of tests made in hospitals and clinics. It has been found that those causes are often tied in with the love life or with situations involving the emotions particularly.

The treatment, then, is not that the cold will leave, but that this particular person is coming into a new experience of peace and fulfillment.

In all treatments, the idea of peace, serenity, tranquillity should be included, because in all conditions requiring healing, including the physical and the financial, this state of mind will be found to be absent; therefore, the manifestation of peace in the patient would mean that his trouble has gone.

HEALING IS OF THE WHOLE PERSON

By this time, the student is coming to see that treatment is not just the waving of a magic wand while he utters a lot of hocus-pocus. It requires intelligent use of the laws of thought and clear reasoning, and it involves more than just ridding a person of his current misery. Treatment effects fundamental changes in his way of looking at life.

It has been noticed that when a person is healed through the spiritual method of the Science of Mind, his whole outlook on life is bettered. He becomes a kindlier, more tolerant, more unselfish person who no longer demands that everything shall revolve about him and his wishes. He begins to meet life as it comes with an ability to adjust himself to it — the sign of an emotionally mature, well-balanced person. His **thought,** as well as his body and affairs, is healed. Thus, the whole man is healed.

SPECIAL HELPS IN STUDY
AND PRACTICAL APPLICATION

These special helps have been carefully prepared to help you get the most out of this course.

Questions on the lesson

I advise that you first study the lesson carefully, then put it aside, write the answers to the questions, and, finally, **check your answers by the lesson.**

Keep the answers as a running commentary on the course **for your own benefit.** At its conclusion, you will find they have become a record of your own growth in consciousness.

1. In spiritual mind healing, what do we treat?

2. Why do we say that nothing can irritate us without our consent?

3. What are the essentials in a treatment for the healing of irritation?

4. What are four practical points in treatment?

5. Explain the spiritual basis for supply.

6. Explain what we mean by the **Principle** of a thing.

7. How can we seek the **Kingdom** of God?

8. What are the essentials in a treatment for supply?

9. Why must we put our attention on what we have to give, not just on what we want?

10. Why do we say that healing is of the whole person?

Collateral reading suggestions

Frederick Bailes: The Healing Power of Balanced Emotions

Hidden Power for Human Problems,
    Chs. 4, 6, and 7

Your Mind Can Heal You, Ch. IX

Ralph Waldo Trine: In Tune With the Infinite, Chs. IV and IX

Practical application

. . . thought-training

Practice seeing back of the visible manifestations of the good things of life the invisible **Infinite Source.**

. . . writing suggestion

Write a treatment for yourself or another person for a specific health condition.

. . . treatment for general good

"The **Lord** is my **Shepherd.** I shall not want" for any good thing.

My mind is at peace, for it is the **Mind** of God, and God's **Mind** could never be disturbed.

I dare to believe that **Life** is loaded with all the good that I desire.
I expect that **Life** is completing itself in me.

Streams of energy flow through every section of my body.

My surroundings are harmonious.
I like the people with whom I live and work, and they like me.

I am amply recompensed for all my efforts.
I give of my best, and it is appreciated.

My chief concern is that I shall be all that I should be this day.

I leave the completing of my good to the **Shepherd,** in whose **Presence** I shall dwell forever.

And it **is** so.

Lesson 10

TREATMENT FOR SPECIFIC CONDITIONS
(continued)

LOVE AND MARRIAGE

"What do I have to give in marriage?"
— we must give happiness in order to receive it

"What do I expect to receive in marriage?"

What you are seeking is seeking you
— no competition for love

Think of all the reasons why it can come true

Sample treatment for those seeking a mate

Our part following treatment

SALESMANSHIP

SECURING NEEDED CAPITAL

RIGHT HOUSING

DESTRUCTIVE HABITS

Excessive drinking

Treating for the excessive drinker

Sample treatment for the excessive drinker

INFINITE MIND IS THE KNOWER

TENTH LESSON
GOALS

To understand the sample treatments
for specific conditions
and the **Principles** underlying them

To make further definite progress
in working out your own treatments
for specific conditions
using those **Principles**

The student by now can readily understand why the body can be healed through spiritual treatment. He has also come to see how his inward negative attitudes can be changed sufficiently for him to draw prosperity into his life. Now we shall see how, through spiritual means, he can draw a life partner, sales from his calls, needed capital for his business, and the right place to live.

This course stresses **Principles,** because the fundamental **Principle,** once grasped, can be applied at a great number of points. By this same **Principle,** he can also draw friendships, right employment, customers to his business, a buyer for his property.

Man can draw into his life anything that he wishes — in reason. Lest this last phrase suggest that we are placing a limitation on the **Law,** we shall explain by saying that we do not think that anyone could grow a green skin on his body because he happens to like that color. But he can bring into his life anything for his growth and happiness.

LOVE AND MARRIAGE

Love and marriage certainly are in the category of experiences that make for growth and happiness. Time after time, I have seen somewhat plain, unattractive persons, both men and women, draw a greatly enriching love into their lives after they have grasped the underlying **Principle** by which this is brought about. We shall now apply that **Principle** to love and marriage.

"What do I have to give in marriage?"

In the first place, the seeker for marital happiness should temporarily turn away from what he or she wants, and approach the situation from the standpoint of what he or she has to offer that will bring completion to the life of another. The person who is seeking a marriage partner might make a list on paper of all his or her abilities and qualities that might appeal to the type of partner desired. The following questions are suggestions for doing this:

Am I home loving, or career minded, or travel minded? Is my disposition good? Can I refrain from snapping back if something is said to displease me? Am I usually cheerful? Do I submerge my wishes to a reasonable extent, or do I always insist on having my own way? Do I keep myself well groomed? Am I extravagant or miserly? Am I gossipy?

Am I warm and affectionate? Do I have initiative? Do I have the ability to make decisions? Am I suspicious or jealous? Am I flirtatious? What subjects am I able to discuss reasonably well? What talents and skills have I? In what stratum of society could I be a worthy part?

— we must give happiness in order to receive it

We must agree with Emerson that no one has the right to anything that is not his by **right of consciousness.** By this we mean that there is a certain level at which we can fulfill the life of another. Quite naturally, we do not wish to marry below this level, for then the other person could never bring us real happiness. On the other hand, we have no right to expect this **Law** to bring us someone so much above our level that our presence would be a constant source of embarrassment or disappointment to him or her. We might be perfectly happy to have **him** — and we are using the pronoun as the common gender — but we might be robbing him of happiness if he should have **us.** This would be imbalance; the **Law** is a law of balance.

Any contract to be fair must equally benefit both parties. Each must willingly continue in it. Each must permanently feel, "I'm glad that I found you of all the people in the world." This is the only basis for a happy marriage.

An illiterate woman might be supremely happy with a college professor, but her constant grammatical blunders might make him ashamed of her. A rough, tough, cursing stevedore might be proudly happy with a refined, sheltered little Dresden china lady, but his every gesture might be an affront to her.

We have a right to draw to us only that which harmonizes with us, and to be drawn only to that person with whom we are well harmonized. Perhaps the best way of putting it would be this: we should treat to draw to us that person whom we enjoy as he is, and whom we have no desire to change; and that person must like us as we are, and have no desire that we be anything different from what we are. To marry with the intention of "reforming" the partner usually ends disastrously.

"What do I expect to receive in marriage?"

We have said earlier that a treatment is a **definite** movement of **Mind.** This **Law** that we use is a law of **reflection.** It reflects, as a mirror, only that which is placed before it. It is not enough to say, "I want to marry." The **Law** can project our wish into form, but what we marry might be quite different from what we really want; therefore, it is well to set down on paper the type of person wanted — his or her qualities, special interests, likes and dislikes, accomplishments in general, and, if a man, his earning power. Do not put down trivialities but only those things that are necessary to perfect harmony. If it doesn't matter whether he is tall or short, or she is blonde or brunette, leave it out.

Divorce judges have told me that the three most common obstacles to happy marriage are drinking, gambling, and infidelity. The mere presence of the first two is not necessarily a barrier provided they are not carried to excess. Many fine people like a cocktail or like to spend a day at the races or an evening at poker; but when these are carried to excess, which is destructive, they can break up a marriage. Some spouses like to join the partner in a moderate amount of these diversions; but if the one seeking a mate is a violent teetotaler or a non-gambler, the treatment should specify that one is attracting a mate not given to these habits at all. There is no question but that infidelity will break up a marriage; so this must be included in the "non-wanted's."

Sometimes a man has previous ties. He may be living apart or with his wife, who, he says, "doesn't understand" him. Know now that this sort of love affair is a dead-end street.

Another tie that may bind either a man or a woman is children by a former marriage. A person may be so much a slave to the children that a spouse must always take second place. This is a frequent cause of marital unhappiness. Normal, balanced ties with the children are admirable, and if the new spouse can establish warm relationships with the children, the marriage is strengthened; if the children resent the new partner, the marriage can be destroyed.

A third tie that should be considered is inordinate subjection to a parent. Sometimes a mother — or, in rarer cases, a father — has kept the child so tied to the apron strings that the parent comes before the spouse.

On our paper, therefore, should be a statement to the effect that there are no previous ties that take precedence over our marriage tie.

To sum it up, the two lists that we have made should include all those essentials for a happy and balanced marriage with emphasis on these: one person with the ability to provide for the up-keep of the home, the other with the ability to make that home a real home, both with dispositions and mental levels that harmonize with each other.

What you are seeking is seeking you

The next paragraph, which touches on fundamentals taken up in previous lessons, may seem at first glance to have no place just here; but since they have to do with the "why" and the "how" of manifestations, it is well that the seeker be reminded of them at this point. Their application to companionship in marriage will follow.

The student advanced this far knows that everything — past, present, and future — is now floating in that stream of consciousness that we call **Infinite Mind.** We do not so much originate thought as we register thought that already is in **Infinite Mind.** All future inventions are already known in that **Mind** long before human "inventors" grope their uncertain way toward them. When a man "invents," or a scientist makes a new "discovery," it merely means that these persons are sensitive enough in that department of their thinking to register ideas that are carried along in the river of **Infinite Mind.**

Now to get back to our seeker for a mate who asks, "Why have I desired this particular sort of person whose description I have put down on paper?" The answer is, "Because someone, somewhere, of exactly this **type** is wishing that he (common gender) could meet someone just like me. He is not attracted to those in his immediate environment, and wishes that a person of my appearance and personality might come his way. Then he would marry."

This does not mean if you are a woman that you are more beautiful or younger or more mature, or if you are a man that you are a better provider than others. It simply means that the tie that binds two together is like an invisible thread running through you and this **type** of person. The fact that you are attracted to a person having the qualities that you have outlined indicates that you are intuitively in harmony with that sort of person; therefore, others of a different **type** leave you cold. Your picture of the ideal is, then, your response to his call, and his picture of his ideal is his answer to your desire.

The **Infinite Mind** is ceaselessly separating that which is not in harmony, and drawing together that which is in harmony. This is the lesson of chemistry, biology, and all the other sciences. It is true also in the mental and spiritual field. The word "affinity" has been degraded to the position of an illicit relationship, but in its noblest sense there are affinities that make for the perfect marriage. They are the result of the intelligent approach to this problem, made through the Science of Mind, by two individuals who understand the **Principle.**

The future mate may be thousands of miles away at this moment. That does not matter. **Omnipresence** knows exactly where he (she) is, and, when properly approached, will bring the two together. The seeker's province is to keep his thought clear and decisive on this point. It is the function of **Infinite Creative Mind** to **open the channels** and **provide the means.**

This answers the question that sometimes arises, "Is it right to treat that a certain person will fall in love with us?" I shall, however, be explicit.

In the Science of Mind, we do not do this because it savors of coercion and hypnotism. Moreover, it is to be remembered that we do not fall in love with a person so much as with a **type.** We have said that there seems to be an invisible thread running through life that draws certain **types** of persons toward each other. Any happily married person could have married any one of ten thousand individuals, and would have been just as happy. But those ten thousand would have had the same hidden something that is the basis of true, mutual appeal. For example, if we had lived in Finland, we never would have met the present partner, but could have been equally happy with one of the right **type** found there.

— no competition for love

One of the things the Science of Mind approach does is to remove all sense of competition. We are never in competition with anyone whom we might consider as having more appeal than we have. One has only to look about at his friends to know that beauty, without a doubt, must be "in the eye of the beholder." There must be some invisible bond holding many couples together because nothing on the exterior could account for some unions; yet they are highly satisfactory.

There is someone who will see us as the ideal, and whom we shall see as the ideal. And there is **no competition.**

Think of all the reasons why it can come true

The Reasoning Method of treatment has usually been found best for drawing love and marriage, because the seeker very often has to reverse his past ways of looking at his desire, and build an entirely new type of consciousness to attain his end.

I am therefore going to repeat something that I said earlier: One of the fundamental reasons why the good we long for does not come to us is because, as soon as we desire it, we immediately begin to think of all the reasons why it cannot come true. This negative attitude effectually blocks the channels through which our good might come to us.

Now, in our new attitude, we shall cultivate the habit of thinking of **all the reasons why it can come true.** Those negative reasons, which are so easy to find, we quickly place in the background and forget. We **choose** to draw into the foreground only the positive **reasons why our desire can come to pass.** This is highly important. **Nothing in the universe denies us our good but we ourselves.**

The woman seeking a mate must also break away from the general thought of those who negatively discuss such matters. How often do we hear, "There are three women to every man," or "Men of my (middle) age want young girls." While these statements are true only to those who believe them, a lie believed will act as if it were the truth. As long as a woman parrots these statements, she is holding her good away from her. To bolster

141

the Reasoning Step in treatment, read the vital statistics columns in the papers and see how many women of your years appear there. This will help remove this false barrier.

Sample treatment for those seeking a mate

The treatment should be somewhat as follows:

I know that I am an extension of **Infinite Mind;** therefore, what is true of it is also true of me. It is never separated from its good, nor does it ever experience any incompleteness at any point in its experience.

My incompleteness has been a false experience, growing out of my false belief about myself and about life. I now reverse my belief, and this word is the expression of my new belief.

I am fully conscious of my own **true worth,** and those I meet are likewise conscious of it. I know that somewhere there is someone who needs and wants me as much as I do him (her) and who will never be fully contented in life until I become a part of the completed circle. He (She) needs me to make a completely rounded life.

This person is thus and so (enumerating the qualities on the paper) and hungers for someone with these qualities (your own on the paper). Our coming together will be the richest fulfillment of life for both of us, for each likes and enjoys the other just as he (she) is.

Infinite Mind knows where each is, and is even now moving beneath the surface to bring us together. I leave it entirely to the **Infinite,** knowing that at this moment the hidden currents of its activity are in motion to this end.

Thus I release my word completely to that **Mind** which unites those who are attuned to each other. It knows the ways and means. I know that it has brought together every happy couple who have ever been united, that it has every eligible person in its thought, and that my quiet expectation is the signal for it to move into action. It knows only completeness; therefore, it is completing two lives by making them one. And it **is** so.

Our part following treatment

Our treatment, therefore, leaves to **Infinite Mind** the bringing to us of the particular individual. Since happiness in marriage must be equal on both sides, **Infinite Mind** does not specialize on a particular person we might select, because as we said before, while we might be very happy with him, he might have good reasons for not finding happiness with us.

This does not mean that we must be recessive, nor does it prevent our making ourselves attractive to a particular person. We may be as attractive as we can, provided we are not putting on a veneer. It is well to remember that it is sincerity, and not tricks, that has the greatest permanent appeal, whether it be in woman or in man.

To the woman who works where all the men are married or where there are few men or no men, or who says, "I never go anywhere where I meet eligible men," we say that these seeming barriers are no barriers to **Infinite Mind.** And since it is the work of **Infinite Mind,** and not herself, to bring together that which is in harmony, there is no reason why she should not meet eligible men anywhere she goes or at any gathering she attends. Let her cultivate an **inner** sense of quiet expectancy. But never, never let undue eagerness show in her manner.

I could have devoted all this space to relating many cases in my files of people who have happily married long after their friends had given up hope of their doing so; however, I felt it would be of more benefit to the student to outline the method by which these persons were helped to rearrange their thoughts, and thus draw their happiness to them. But this we can state emphatically without going into details: no one is too unbeautiful or too old or too unattractive externally to draw his (her) mate unless he (she) holds a fixed belief along these lines.

SALESMANSHIP

The **Principle** here for the salesman is that a sale must not be just something that **he** wants. His prospect must want to buy or to be shown that it is to his advantage to buy, and he must be equally satisfied after he has bought. True, the salesman works because he wants the commission, but until he **sees his sale as a service to the other fellow,** he will not be a great salesman nor a scientific salesman.

He must treat to know that there are thousands upon thousands of persons, not satisfied with what they now have, who want and are ready to buy the goods that he has to sell. They may never have heard of his merchandise or services, but they have an unrecognized hunger for them; and when the salesman presents his goods to them, something within them will make them glad to get what he has to offer.

SECURING NEEDED CAPITAL

To the person who needs capital for his business, we say, start to build the inward conviction that somewhere there is someone who lives from investments and who wishes he knew where there is a sound place to invest his money.

143

Many persons who were either starting or expanding their business have come to me for treatment along this line, persons who for months had unsuccessfully knocked on doors and butted their heads against brick walls trying to raise the necessary capital. Once they had learned the truly scientific way of arranging their thought-life, they found doors to capital swinging open, often before they had knocked.

RIGHT HOUSING

Whether there is a housing shortage or not, every person wants the right place to live. The seeker for right housing can know this: that there is a house or an apartment that has never been properly lived in until he lives in it; that the owner either knowingly or unknowingly wants his type of person for a tenant; that the locality is just what he likes; that the price is within his financial range; that the neighbors are easy to live with; that the rooms are arranged to suit his purpose; and any other detail that he thinks necessary.

Infinite Mind knows where that place is, and when we release our desire to it, a movement starts within **Mind** to open up the channels for the bringing together of place and tenant.

As we have stressed before, we stress again, that the important thing for the student to grasp is the **Principle.** The applications of the **Principle** are many. We might liken it to a vacuum cleaner, which works according to a certain principle of electricity, and to which many kinds of attachments can be adjusted. Once a person knows how to plug it in and turn the switch, it is simply a matter of **choice** as to which attachment he will use.

DESTRUCTIVE HABITS

Now we turn to another **Principle.** We shall apply it to only one destructive habit, but the student may apply it to any of the destructive habits.

Excessive drinking

It is now well established that excessive drinking is an emotional rather than a physical, illness. It invariably springs from a conscious or unconscious sense of inadequacy at one or more points in the life. The uncontrolled drinker is first a person with a sense of defeat who is running away from his recognition of his insufficiency somewhere although he might be quite successful financially.

Man was created for winning, not losing. When he wins, he is in tune with **Life** and with the **Source** of **Life.** All the generations of overcomers from whom he has descended speak to him in his blood, brain, and nervous system. Man is of noble ancestry, therefore cannot stand the humiliation that failure brings. Even the little child undergoes painful feelings of shame and humiliation when scolded or scorned. Men have waited years to kill someone who has humiliated them. The expression, "I was so mortified I could have died" is truer than appears.

Drinking raises one's ego. After a few drinks, the mousy man, who has always failed to assert himself, becomes noisy and quarrelsome, and sometimes tries to take the officer's club away from him. He may become boastful, relating as true experiences that which is only dreamy fantasy. Thus alcohol takes away the bitter awareness of failure, making him a "king for a day" in a make-believe sense. He may play God by giving money away.

More drinks carry him beyond this stage of false self-sufficiency into one in which his sense of failure will not down. Sober, he would be ashamed to be seen crying, but now, with his inhibitions removed, he moves into a "crying jag," in which his **deeper mind** unashamedly admits what he has consciously avoided recognizing — his failure. In this stage, he sometimes talks of taking his life, which supports our statements in the second paragraph under this heading.

This death wish is carried out vicariously in the terminal stage of drinking, in which he "passes out." Further drinking has carried him past the stage of boasting, self-pity, crying, shame. He loses interest in his surroundings and sinks slowly into oblivion, the temporary equivalent of death. But the entire cycle has been negative, starting with a sense of defeat and ending in a complete running away from it. Nothing has been solved.

Treating for the excessive drinker

If one's **mind** can be elevated to the consciousness of power and self-sufficiency under the influence of alcohol, a narcotic, it can be raised to that same level without the narcotic, for drugs do not create power; they merely uncover **powers that already are a part of one's mental make-up.** Alcohol provides pictures of self-sufficiency. The **mind** has other material capable of producing the same pictures of **adequacy** without alcohol.

Our previous lessons have shown that **man is in the small what God is in the large,** that all the **Infinite adequacy** is in man, and that when he cultivates a sense of **oneness** with the **Infinite,** the nature and powers of the **Infinite** flow through him. It is a striking fact that there is seldom a true deliverance from excessive drinking unless this **union of God and man** is stressed. No one ever defeats alcohol by gritting his teeth and fighting furiously against it. He whips it by turning toward **Something** more potent and more desirable.

Sample treatment for the excessive drinker

A treatment that has proved effective is along these lines:

John Smith, 1111 Blank Road, Townville, is a part of that **Infinite Person,** whose roots are in eternity. He partakes of the nature of the **Infinite,** which has never been blocked nor defeated at any point in its experience. He is completely **adequate** to meet life at any point without any false stimulation.

He is now a "God-intoxicated" person, filled with a sense of unbreakable **oneness** with the **Infinite.** God's thoughts are his thoughts. There is no room for failure thoughts, for he is one with all the currents of **Life.**

He does not have to fight liquor. He simply does not respond to its appeal. His desire for it has vanished in his new-found **oneness** with **Infinite Wisdom** and **Power.** He is dead to it because he is alive to the **Infinite** within him.

Life has a new meaning for him. He penetrates deeper into the heart and reality of things. He is **united** with all that contains beauty, and is mentally and emotionally separated from everything that is ugly or destructive. Life has purpose for him. He sees it stretching ahead, leading him into self-fulfillment, usefulness, satisfactory achievement.

I speak my word for John Smith, knowing that the galleries of his **mind** are filled with pictures of those things that are "lovely, noble, pure, and of good report," and that it is not he, but the Father within him that doeth the work.

This is my highest thought for John Smith, and I release it completely to **Infinite Mind,** knowing as I do that it **is** so.

INFINITE MIND IS THE KNOWER

Never forget that **Infinite Mind** is the **Knower.** It knows where all persons, places, and things that are in harmony with one another are. It would always bring them together were it not for man's ignorance. Man blocks the channels by which his good might come to him by building mental pictures of the extreme difficulty of raising money or finding a place to live or getting the right job or selling enough customers. It knows how to lift man to the highest level of adequacy where he is able to meet life at any point.

Man needs to know that he has a **Silent Partner,** who is a better real estate agent than the best human living, a more intelligent capital raiser than the best promoter, a better physician than the most skillful doctor, a better intermediary than the most successful marriage broker, who can make one more adequate than the most powerful drug. This **Partner** is always ready to bring things to completion. The only thing that can stop this **Partner** from doing so is man's own obstructive **thought.**

This **Knower** is the **Opener** of gates, the **Dissolver** of problems. Nothing is too insignificant for its attention, nothing too hard for its power, nothing too intricate for its skill. Every second of every hour it works, ceaselessly weaving the pattern of our **thoughts** into the pattern of our affairs. But it can work only with the threads of **thought** we give it.

Our business, therefore, is not to sit despondently wishing or praying that our negative conditions will change, but to **select** positive, constructive threads of **thought, release** them to **Infinite Mind,** then leave the rest to the one **Creative Agency** that can bring about a conclusion that is satisfactory and fair to everyone concerned, and that can deliver one from any destructive habit.

SPECIAL HELPS IN STUDY
AND PRACTICAL APPLICATION

These special helps have been carefully prepared to help you get the most out of this course.

Questions on the lesson

I advise that you first study the lesson carefully, then put it aside, write the answers to the questions, and, finally, **check your answers by the lesson.**

Keep the answers as a running commentary on the course **for your own benefit.** At its conclusion, you will find they have become a record of your own growth in consciousness.

1. Why do we stress **Principles** in this course?

2. What is the first step in drawing a life partner or in any situation in which one expects to receive from another?

3. Why should we be definite in what we expect to receive from another in marriage?

4. Explain, "What you are seeking is seeking you."

5. Why is it important that we think of all the reasons why a good thing should come true?

6. What are the essentials in a treatment for love and marriage?

7. How must a salesman consider his sale in relation to the buyer?

8. What are the main points to include in a treatment for right housing?

9. What are the essentials in a treatment for excessive drinking?

10. What is the significance for us in treatment that **Infinite Mind** is the **Knower?**

Collateral reading suggestions

Frederick Bailes: Hidden Power for Human Problems, Chs. 8, 9, and 10

"How to Get Along With Troublesome People"

Kahlil Gibran: The Prophet
"On Love," "On Marriage," "On Giving," "On Work," "On Houses," "On Buying and Selling," "On Friendship"

Practical application

. . . thought-training

Practice giving of your thought.

Give on the mental level by kindly words to others and considerate attention to what they are saying.

Give on the spiritual level by good thoughts about them either in specific treatment or in casual thought.

. . . writing suggestion

Write a treatment for yourself or another person for some specific condition, using one of the **Principles** illustrated in this lesson.

. . . a treatment for general good

This day I stand at the door of limitless opportunity.

Life beckons to me and smiles encouragement.

Life flows through me, touching my body with its **Infinite Healing Presence** and blotting out everything unlike itself.

Life pours itself through my business this day, bringing increase of opportunity to serve and to be recompensed.

My home and my loved ones are blessed this day and surrounded by right action.

Peace, health, and happiness rule all my experiences this day, this week, this year.

I release my word to **Infinite Mind** and relax in the knowledge that —

— it **is** so.

Lesson 11

PRACTICAL AIDS IN TREATMENT

GENERAL TREATMENT REMINDERS

Quality and quantity of belief

— instantaneous healing

Qualities of the good practitioner

THE "DISSOLVING" METHOD

THE "REFUSAL" METHOD

THE "ESCALATOR" METHOD

THE "FOCAL" METHOD

THE "REPLACEMENT" METHOD

THE "ARCHITECT" METHOD

ELEVENTH LESSON
GOALS

To understand the practical aids
    in treatment

To make definite progress
    in working out
        your own practical aids

In this lesson, we shall discuss several aids in treatment that I have found effective over the almost fifty years that I have helped to perfect the Science of Mind method of dealing with life. There will be moments in the student's healing work when his treatment seems to be getting nowhere, and it is then that he will find invaluable the dramatization of some enlightening point that may occur to him in treatment and that will break the mental block that has delayed the healing. I have used those detailed in this lesson on many thousands of persons and in the great majority of cases with good success.

GENERAL TREATMENT REMINDERS

Quality and quantity of belief

Before we take up these aids, however, it is well to emphasize the fact that to heal any condition — whether it relates to health, finance, employment, marital happiness, or any other state — it is imperative that the student turn away from the false to concentrate his focus of attention on the correct **belief.** Whether a healing is gradual or instantaneous depends entirely on the speed with which he can substitute the new viewpoint for the old.

— instantaneous healing

During our Sunday morning services, where a high state of consciousness was attained by the thousands who attended, healings were frequently instantaneous. Scarcely a service passed but that someone approached me to say something like this: "This is my first Sunday here, and a persistent headache (or bodily pain) that I have had for weeks completely disappeared while you were speaking. Could it actually be cured in such a short time?"

The answer is that the greatest Authority on this **Law** once said, "It is done unto you **as** you believe." "As" refers to quality and quantity. It means the way we **believe.** When the conviction of the **Power** outweighs the fear of the condition, both the quality and the quantity of the **belief** are satisfactory, and the healing occurs. Moreover, it can happen in the twinkling of an eye. These are called instantaneous healings. Develop your expectancy of them. They can happen to you.

Men who have not drawn a sober breath nor earned an honest dollar in years have staggered into rescue missions and have had the whole course of their lives changed in a few minutes' time. Somehow, a single illuminating thought has penetrated the alcoholic mists beclouding their minds and so changed the focus of their **belief** that they have become useful and respected citizens. This changed **belief** has been brought about in a few minutes' time.

153

It is by this change of focus that healing occurs in the Science of Mind method. Actually, there are no healers as such. The one giving a treatment does not heal the person for whom he treats. But he does change his own false **belief** about that person's condition, and in so doing tunes in on the **Principle,** to which all have access and which accomplishes the healing.

Qualities of the good practitioner

We have previously stressed the fact that in Science of Mind treatment there are two extremes to be avoided. One is self-depreciation; the other, self-aggrandizement. Either will prevent satisfactory results.

Self-depreciation can grow out of one's fear that he has not sufficient education. Some of the most successful practitioners have had a very limited formal education, but their **consciousness** of the **Power** of the **Infinite** is very strong. Some of high scholastic attainments, on the other hand, fail in treatment because of a weak healing **consciousness.**

Anyone who constantly thinks, "I am not good enough," will be unable to get satisfactory results as long as this dominates his thinking. This is not because of his lack of "goodness" but because of his belief about this real or supposed lack. If goodness were a prerequisite, there would be little healing since none of us has lived consistently on as high a level as he would desire. Truth unchecked, however, can operate surprisingly through very imperfect channels, for it is the truth, not the agent, which sets the person free. The **Power** is in the **Healing Presence;** the practitioner is only the channel through which it operates.

At the other extreme is he who thinks or speaks of himself as a "good healer." True, he may see excellent results coming from his treatment, but he is mistaken in thinking that it is himself who heals. One is not a "good illuminator" because he turns on a switch. It is the law of electricity that banishes the darkness by bringing the light.

The moment we interpose anything between the **Power** and the patient, it becomes a hindrance. The belief in either our "goodness" or our "badness" can obstruct; in fact, anything that distracts our attention from the real healing **Agent** can become a barrier. The one who treats successfully remains **humble;** yet he is supremely confident of the **Power** by which the healing is accomplished. This is a fine point that should be well established in the student's mind. The greatest Practitioner who ever lived said, "Of myself, I can do nothing"; this was his **humility.** It was his **confidence** that added, "The Father in me, He it is that doeth the works."

154

THE "DISSOLVING" METHOD

I was once treating for a woman for the removal of a serious condition. Every few days she would telephone to report that she was no better. It was one of those rare cases that one sometimes encounters in which, despite the best efforts of the practitioner, no improvement shows. The Analytical Method quite evidently had failed to uncover the blockage in thought; yet the one who treated knew there are no incurable diseases, and that somewhere there must be an answer to the problem.

At home, after a busy day at the office, I sometimes relaxed before dinner by watching the slow, easy movements of the tropical fish in a large rectangular aquarium. On this particular evening, in reaching under water to move a piece of coral on the bottom, I noticed a crystal-clear streak follow where my hand had touched the glass side of the tank as I withdrew it.

The light shining through the water had given the impression that the tank was clean. But now I saw there was a film of scum on the glass; and faced with the task of removing water, plants, and fish in order to clean the aquarium, I found myself wishing there were some harmless solvent that could be sprinkled on the surface and that would melt away all film and dirt as it slowly sank to the bottom.

It was in that instant that the thought flashed into my mind: "This is exactly what is needed in this woman's case. You have been trying to analyze and wash away the 'film' without result. Why not sit back, relax, and watch the **Infinite Healing Solvent** move slowly through every cell of her body, neutralizing each last remnant of her disordered thought?"

A day or two later came the call reporting great improvement, and in a short while the condition had disappeared completely. This is not to deny the efficacy of the Analytical Method; but when one way seems not to bring good results, one may switch with success to another such as this which I call the "dissolving" treatment.

THE "REFUSAL" METHOD

One day a man came to the office with an ugly looking rash that had broken out all over his body. He said that even after several months of medication, diet, etc., dermatologists had been unable to help him; and he added, "This thing has got me down. I'm really afraid. I try to keep my thought right, but even in my most hopeful moments, it persists."

My answer was, "Suppose a man came to your door right now with an elephant. Suppose he told you he was disbanding his circus, and had decided to give you this tremendous beast. You reply that you do not want the animal, but he insists that he is leaving it with you just the same. You then tell the man that you have not solicited this doubtful gift, nor have you any place to house it, and if he persists in the matter, you have the right to do the final thing and say, 'I refuse to accept or take delivery of this thing you offer.' Whereupon, you may close the door in his face, and under the law he is compelled to take the unwelcome beast away."

Precisely the same thing can be done with an unwanted condition. While it is true that we treat the thought rather than the condition, there are times when we must be very positive in regard to the condition; and we can be sure that in so doing, we are backed up by mental **Law.**

We may say this:

I did not consciously ask for this condition, nor will I accept it. It is not a part of me. No place in my body was provided to house such a thing; therefore I refuse it. I shut the door of my consciousness in its face, for I know that "To them that receive Him [**Infinite Wisdom**], He gives power to become [in their bodies also] the sons of God."

The man caught the idea. Within twenty-four hours, his trouble had disappeared, for, having freed himself of the elephantine fear of the condition, the **Power** had an opportunity to do its work, and the healing was accomplished.

THE "ESCALATOR" METHOD

The manner in which impersonal **Law** can take us to any one of many diverse manifestations is exemplified by the department store escalator. All day long, person after person steps onto it on his way to the department where he will find the merchandise he wants. The escalator is unaware of what they seek, and moves only in a prescribed direction that will carry anyone to the level he determines.

In this proceeding, however, the person must first exercise **selection** in deciding on what level he will find the goods he seeks. He must also use **initiative,** taking the necessary steps to place his feet on the moving stairs. The escalator will not reach out and drag him aboard, nor will it wait a single instant; it just keeps moving upward. Once the person steps aboard, however, it becomes his servant with full responsibility to carry him to the higher level he has **selected.**

I outlined the escalator method to a young student who had tried repeatedly to get into a line of work for which he was well prepared and very much wanted to enter. He had never been able to get past secretaries, his letters had gone unanswered, and he was discouraged and doubtful that he knew enough about the **Law** to use it.

During our talk, the young man began to see that it was not necessary for him to know how the escalator worked. The important thing was that once he had stepped aboard, it knew how to transport him to the upper floor. Presently, he gave his own treatment, saying something like this:

> **Infinite Mind,** I want just one interview with someone who is able to give me a job in the line of work for which I am prepared. You know how to take me to it. I don't care how you do it just so long as I can have it. See, I am putting my foot on the escalator now! I am relying on you to bring this meeting about. I know I don't have to struggle to reach that level. You are taking me there.

On Saturday afternoons, it had been this young man's custom to caddy at the country club; and on the following Saturday when an influential man in this work was, for the first time, a guest at the club, our young fellow was assigned to caddy for him. The man was one of a foursome, but from time to time he chatted with his alert and personable caddy; and before the eighteen holes were played, the young man had had his longed-for interview and had landed a job.

Our responsibility is to gain the consciousness of completion. It is the responsibility of **Infinite Mind** to find the way to open the door.

THE "FOCAL" METHOD

A case in which there was an instantaneous healing was treated in the following manner:

> In my treatment, I began to think of the man I was treating for as sitting alone in the center of a room in his home. I began then to think of healing rays of light that flowed downward from the molding near the room's ceiling, and upward from the molding around the floor's edge, so there was not one spot in the room that was not flooded with rays; and all of these rays converged upon the man, coming to a focal point in him with terrific healing power.

> In order not to think of these as earthly rays of physical origin, I then declared them to be totally invisible, having the **Life** of **Spirit,** and there to be nothing in the man's consciousness or body that was able to resist their positive **Power.** Then, as I have said, the change was brought about instantaneously, and the man was healed.

THE "REPLACEMENT" METHOD

There are times when, in the midst of other duties, the practitioner is called upon for an emergency treatment; and excellent results have often followed the use of this method:

The practitioner begins with an image of the person being treated for. Naturally, this is a picture of the physical man; but soon the mind of the one who treats releases the physical impression so that it gradually recedes and disappears, and in its place he allows to emerge a perfect circle or sphere. This circle he conceives to be the image of perfection, and since there are no features, face, or form to intrude, he is able quickly and easily to treat impersonally with his mind stayed on the **Absolute** of **Perfection,** from which **Source** comes all healing.

THE "ARCHITECT" METHOD

It is true that we do not treat the physical body as such. Rather, we treat the underlying **thought.** But there are times when the student will find the following method valuable:

Consider the beginning of a human life — a male and a female cell fused into one. At the moment of fusion are sealed up in that cell all the inherited characteristics that the emerging man will manifest. Nothing more can now be added. The **Infinite** sees the adult man in the cell. The man is in the cell, all organs completed, though as yet his tissues are only ideas.

From that one cell, but eventually composed of as many as fifty trillion cells as an adult, the infant will ultimately emerge. **Infinite Intelligence** will cause to evolve only what was in that primary cell. In one sense, the entire man is unfolded from that cell, where he was hidden with all his inherited characteristics at conception. **Infinite Mind** knows the mechanics of building any sort of cell, never having to stop and wonder what to do next. It needs nothing but a pattern to follow, a concept to be turned into protoplasm. It moves surely and with certainty, completing the entire structure in approximately two hundred eighty days.

Every organ and every cell in man's body is a separate concept held in **Infinite Mind.** All of God's concepts are perfect and changeless; therefore, any person believing himself to be ill is looking at himself in a manner unlike the one in which the **Infinite** regards him. "Man looketh on the outward appearance, but the Lord looketh on the heart [origin]."

Mind is at this moment creating untold billions of cells, not only in hundreds of thousands of unborn children, but also for the repair and upkeep of all ages in all manifested bodies. It is never confused. It knows what to do and is willing and eager to do it; therefore, we turn away from the seeming incurability of any condition, knowing that it is only an outward appearance. We say something like this:

> The **Intelligence** that built this structure knows exactly what to do to reconstruct it. It is now rebuilding while I, the practitioner, let my **thought** coincide with the original **Thought** of the **Infinite.** I am now looking on the cell, the spiritual concept, the original building, seeing it as perfect as does God, whose concept of its perfection has never changed.

In the treatment just outlined, we see that in **Reality** there is nothing to heal. Our work is only to correct the tendency to look at the outer effect, thus changing our viewpoint to focus on inner **Cause,** which is eternally perfect. There will be an outer change, but the practitioner is not primarily concerned with it, nor is he responsible for it, although he welcomes it as much as the patient does.

In the "Architect" Method of treatment, it can be clearly seen that the healing is not so much a process as it is a revelation of the truth about man. Whatever process is involved belongs entirely in the province of **Infinite Intelligence,** and consists only in the actual physical alteration of the cells to manifest their perfection.

You are now completing the eleventh lesson of our course and the last of the five lessons specifically on the technique of treatment. Our closing lesson will be on consciousness, which underlies all healing and which I have emphasized throughout these lessons.

MAN, KNOW THYSELF
MAN AS A THREE-STORIED BEING

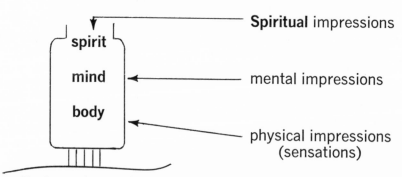

Spiritual impressions

mental impressions

physical impressions
(sensations)

Body rests on the earth on the five "legs" of the senses, and receives physical impressions, or sensations.

The five "legs" give man contact with material things.

He can, if he wishes, live on this level with virtually no mental life.

But if he does, his life narrows down as he grows older, and he feels forlorn and lost.

Mind receives mental impressions from the intellect and the emotions.

He can withdraw from the world with a book and delve into some subject.

He can probe into why and wherefore.

He can perceive beauty in a phrase in literature, a musical composition, a painting, a flower.

As he moves up into this story, he is developing his inner resources, and living a more balanced life.

Spirit receives **Spiritual** impressions, direct knowledge, from "above" without conscious mental processes.

Behind the world that we perceive with the senses and interpret with the **mind** is a vast **Spiritual** world.

Material "things" are only symbols of a world "back of" or "above."

Man's hungers for more of the intangible values of life are his response to **Spiritual** impressions.

They are that "light that lighteth every man that cometh into the world."

When we are giving treatment, our thought should rise above the condition, above the mental analysis, up into the **Spiritual** world.

SPECIAL HELPS IN STUDY
AND PRACTICAL APPLICATION

These special helps have been carefully prepared to help you get the most out of this course.

Questions on the lesson

I advise that you first study the lesson carefully, then put it aside, write the answers to the questions, and, finally, **check your answers by the lesson.**

Keep the answers as a running commentary on the course **for your own benefit.** At its conclusion, you will find they have become a record of your own growth in consciousness.

1. Explain, "It is done unto you as you believe."
2. In treatment, what only do we seek to heal?
3. What are the qualities of the good practitioner?
4. What is the heart of the "Dissolving" Method?
5. What underlies the "Refusal" Method?
6. What characteristic of the **Law** does the "Escalator" Method emphasize?
7. What is the strength of the "Focal" Method?
8. What is the strength of the "Replacement" Method?
9. What is the strength of the "Architect" Method?
10. Explain, "Healing is not so much a process as it is a revelation of the truth about man."

Collateral reading suggestions

Frederick Bailes: Hidden Power for Human Problems, Ch. 13

Your Mind Can Heal You, Ch. IV

Gene Emmet Clark: Let's Talk About You

Ervin Seale: Take Off from Within

Practical application

. . . thought-training

Turn your thought to ways of making the **Infinite Healing Presence** vivid to you in your treatment.

. . . writing suggestion

Write a treatment for yourself or another person for any condition using some special aid of your own.

. . . treatment for general good

This day my soul is caught up in the assurance that the **Infinite** is close at hand, radiant with supreme **Beauty,** the **Beauty of Wholeness.**

It is the **Infinite Healing Presence,** closer to me than my breath.

It is formless, nameless, beyond description or explanation, yet never beyond my personal experience.

It is the **All-in-All.**

Its **Wholeness** is so complete that it blots out all lack and all experience of anything less than the **Whole.**

There is nothing that can stand before it, oppose it, or block its onward sweep.

It throws clear light upon my path, and fills me with serenity, tranquillity, peace.

Easily, effortlessly, I surrender myself this day to **That Which Is Over All and Within All.**

And it **is** so.

Lesson 12

THE HEALING CONSCIOUSNESS

CLEARING THE PATHWAY

No hostilities

No self-pity

No negative discussion

BUILDING THE CONSCIOUSNESS

Recognition of inward compulsion

Willingness to co-operate

A growing awareness of unity

Rising in thought

SPIRIT'S VIEW OF THE UNIVERSE

The masterpiece revealed

Spiritual thinking

— the fruits of spiritual thinking

Spirit sees no obstructions or delays

— **Spirit** sees the end from the beginning

MIND CARRIES OUT THE CREATIVE PROCESS

CONSCIOUSNESS OF OMNIPOTENCE — ALL POWER

FINAL WORD AND BLESSING

TWELFTH LESSON
GOALS

To come into a clearer understanding
of what the healing consciousness is

To make further definite progress
in cultivating the healing consciousness

As the student has made his way through this basic course, it must have become evident that the art of healing consists of something more than a mere knowledge of the techniques.

He must have seen also that **thought** is paramount, and that the practitioner deals with nothing else. It naturally follows that our **thoughts** are tools that the **Infinite Sculptor** uses to liberate the perfect figure that lies hidden in the block of rough stone.

We have said repeatedly that **thoughts** are things. The practitioner is constantly trying to produce things, or results, by the use of his **thought;** therefore, the quality of those things will depend upon the quality of his **thought.** This quality is his **consciousness,** which we spent some time on in Lesson 5, and have touched upon in other lessons. If his **consciousness** be of a limited order, the things that issue from it will be of a limited order. If it be of a high order, the manifestations will be equally high.

Consciousness is not easy to define, nor are the steps into a higher **consciousness** easy to outline. The teacher can lead the student by the hand along the pathway of methods; the student himself is responsible for the development of his **consciousness,** and must take — alone — those last steps that lead him into a high **consciousness.**

Man's **consciousness** is dependent upon his concept of God. All that any of us know of God is what we have experienced of Him. Many persons know a great deal about God, but the practitioner must **know** God directly.

By "God" we mean, of course, the **Infinite Superintending** and **Creating Intelligence** that lies behind and throughout the physical universe.

CLEARING THE PATHWAY

High consciousness is a high state of mind partaking of the qualities of **Spirit;** therefore, if one is to develop it, certain attitudes must be removed from the thought-life.

No hostilities

The first attitudes to go must be envy, jealousy, censoriousness, suspicion, hatred, resentment, and certain kinds of fear. We must be broad enough to know that all men are on the pathway to individual freedom, and that those who seem cruel or wicked are only blind. If those people would come to see more clearly the **Realities** of life, they would cease to be cruel or selfish or heartless; therefore, they are to be pitied, not censured.

It is not hard to forgive when one understands this. We do not hate the hunchback or the person with a clubfoot. We recognize him as one suffering from a deformity, and we are sorry for him.

An ugly disposition is as truly a mental and personality deformity as those physical handicaps; therefore, we forgive.

No self-pity

We have said before that self-pity also must go. It is not only a hindrance; it is a sign that the student has not clearly seen that he alone draws into his life all outer experiences. If these are oppressive, the only place where they could have been fabricated is in the buried centers of his own **deeper mind**. His own **thought-attitude** is responsible. Nothing else has power to bring his troubles upon him.

He does not have to change others, but, positively, he must change himself. When he has done this, he will be agreeably surprised to see how others change toward him, and how he will draw less and less of the disagreeable into his life. He will never again defeat himself by feeling sorry for himself.

No negative discussion

The practitioner will cultivate the habit of not discussing the frailties or meannesses of others. The **Infinite** does not see them; therefore, the practitioner should not see them. This will help him to rise above those resentful feelings that hamper the work of some practitioners. It will help prevent him from taking sides in domestic or legal problems that he is helping to solve. He must remain impartial if he is to help.

This latter is highly necessary in a practitioner. In disputes, he should never treat that someone else will change his conduct, or that another person will do anything. He should treat that everything hidden is being uncovered, and that right action is emerging out of what looks like wrong action so that whatever is just shall come forth into manifestation. Our human judgment may err in taking sides. The **Infinite** never errs.

BUILDING THE CONSCIOUSNESS

There is one **Perfect Consciousness** in the universe — that of the **Infinite.** Man's **consciousness** rises in proportion to his union with the **Infinite Consciousness.** Following are some of the steps that advanced students have taken in making their way up into the rarefied spiritual **consciousness** of **Infinite Spirit:**

Recognition of inward compulsion

There has always been a recognition of the inward pressure of the **Infinite** on man. Every higher aspiration we have ever had, every noble impulse, every desire for a higher level of understanding or of living, is a clear evidence of the inward thrust of the **Infinite** outward.

Willingness to co-operate

There must be a willingness to respond and to co-operate with the **Infinite** in this process of growth and enlargement. The thought of **Infinite Intelligence** is perfect. The selfsame image of perfection is always held deep within man by the **Knower** within him. The way he responds to what life does to him will be the indicator of his response to the image of perfection.

At this stage of man's evolution, it seems impossible for him to achieve absolute perfection in his life. The aim, rather than the attainment, is the chief consideration. His very willingness to let the **Absolute** work itself out through him is the key to his growth. He starts to picture to himself the characteristics of the **Infinite Thinking,** and endeavors to allow these to express themselves through him, knowing that he grows through surrender to them.

A growing awareness of unity

There is no "otherness" in the universe. One of the basic ideas that the **Infinite** must evidently hold is that there is nothing but itself in the universe. All is from God and of God. The entire universe and every tiniest part is some part of God. There can, therefore, be no real conflict between them or within them.

The belief in duality must be wiped out and replaced with a belief in **unity.** Here begins the fundamental state in building **consciousness.** We have covered this to a certain degree in a previous lesson, but it is such an important subject that it needs amplification.

Since there is no "otherness," the **Infinite** can never see the ugly, the distorted, the failing, the inharmonious, the ill, the wretched, that man's dual vision constantly sees. God is "of purer eyes than to behold evil." This being so, the practitioner must cultivate the habit of denying the **Reality** of those negative experiences he treats for, of closing his eyes to them as much as he can, and of seeing that what God has made is "very good." Negative experiences may be apparently real in the experience, yet not in ultimate **Reality.**

Rising in thought

It is essential that the student keep the picture of the unchangeability of the **Originating Intelligence.** It stands back of the universe like a great **Beacon** sending its **Beam** of **Perfect Thinking** throughout the universe. It cannot lower its **Beam** to anything less than perfection, for then it would not be perfect.

Man's purpose in living is to **raise his level of thinking** to the height of this **Beacon.** As long as he grovels in his own weaknesses and resentments, his beam of thought is far below the resistless **Beam** of God's perfection. He may wring his hands and cry for help, but the heavens seem completely unresponsive to him.

Man has the powers of **selection** and **initiative,** which are part of his nature as they are of God's nature. The response to his "prayer" or "treatment" comes from **choosing** definitely to turn his eyes away from his own weaknesses, stop bewailing his imperfections, and **rise in thought** to his oneness with that **Perfect Beam.**

When he does this, his thought is immediately infiltrated by, and saturated with, this **Beam** of God's **Perfect Thinking,** and by the law of unification the **Perfect Beam** of **Infinite Power** flows through his chosen picture and condenses it into form.

It might be incorrect to call this an answer to prayer, for it is the nature of the **Beacon** that we call "God" to flow through and convert into form any picture that we have **selected** as being the desire of our hearts.

SPIRIT'S VIEW OF THE UNIVERSE

We have pointed out several times that we should not look upon the appearance, but upon the heart—the heart and core of perfection. For this reason, we should constantly remember that **Spirit** sees no distortion, and we must see none. **Spirit** sees no malignancy, no debts, no quarrels. Always and forever, it sees everything as "very good." The spiritual **consciousness** aligns itself with **Spirit's** viewing of the universe.

Spirit sees only **Life,** always in the **Beauty of Holiness,** which means the **Beauty of Wholeness.** Beauty is symmetry, without distortion or imbalance. Disease is imbalance. All problems are imbalance. **Spirit** ses all things always in one perfect equilibrium.

The practitioner cultivates the ability to deny what seems most real to the eye of the senses, and to penetrate deeper to the true heart of the matter, which is the unchanging and unfailing continuity of the original image of perfection.

The masterpiece revealed

Perhaps an illustration from the world of art will, in a way, make clearer the unchanging and unfailing continuity of the original image of perfection.

Art dealers have sometimes resorted to a ruse to get a masterpiece out of Europe. Since governments wishing to keep certain priceless paintings in the land of their origin have forbidden their export, a crafty dealer has taken such a masterpiece to a sixth-rate artist, had him daub a mediocre picture over the original, and then presented it for export.

Until the system was discovered, many valuable works of art came to this country in this way. Upon arrival here, they were placed in the hands of a person who knew how to restore the original by gently rubbing with oils. With infinite care, the daub was gradually rubbed away until the masterpiece stood forth once more in all its original beauty.

The practitioner must always **know** that beneath the surface daub of sin, illness, poverty, and misery lies the original **Masterpiece.** Thus his trained **thought** removes the deceptive surface and lets the original creation stand forth.

But, just as the restorer cannot create a masterpiece but only restore it, so the practitioner cannot create perfection but only uncover it. Before he can do this, however, he must be sure it lies beneath the surface appearance. This is spiritual thinking.

Spiritual thinking

Normal people shy away from anything that savors of sanctimoniousness, "holiness," or "otherworldliness." Many have the idea that in order to think spiritually, they must become a little peculiar. As a matter of fact, there are no more normal persons in the world than truly spiritual thinkers, for they see things in perspective. They see all outward things as real in experience, and as experiences to shun or enjoy; but they see also the unreality of everything but the eternal values. They know that man's real world is his inner world of ideas.

They are not intimidated by so-called incurable diseases, knowing them to be only the ugly daub superimposed upon the real **Beauty of Wholeness.** Neither are they caught up by the false values of the material. They recognize that money (seen) grows out of wealth (unseen). They know the frightening experiences of life to be only **thought**-forms that they themselves or their fellows have created. Constantly, their spiritual vision pierces the veil of the material and penetrates to the eternal **Realities,** allowing these to come forth.

Spiritual thinkers are none the less human in their physical appetites and feelings, but they invest even these with the deeper beauty of the spiritual, thus enhancing their pleasures without ever being entrapped or enslaved by them. The chief aspect of this spiritual view of life is that everything is kept in its proper place, and nothing assumes undue proportions. Only thus can they keep themselves "unspotted from the world," even while walking in the world — "in the world but not of it."

— the fruits of spiritual thinking

Spiritual thinkers can be the instruments of healing because trouble, which is real and pressing to others, is seen by them as a chimera, which has no real existence, no real power, no real effect, and no valid ground for continued existence. They are thus able to declare its nothingness. Since disease and other miseries are basically **thought,** set and molded into form, spiritual thinkers know that their enlightened **thought** can dissolve the unwanted form, and set up a perfect **thought**-pattern, which the **Infinite Creative Mind** will follow to bring the perfect form into manifestation.

We have said that the spiritually minded man is a normal and practical man. Now, there is nothing practical about bad or destructive habits, and the student of the Science of Mind will find as he progresses that such habits will drop away from him naturally and easily, not through will power but because he loses all desire to continue what is obviously a handicap to him; but the dropping away will be the effect, not the cause of his spiritual advancement.

A person may never have had the faintest impulse toward crime or infidelity; he may also be free from such habits as drinking, smoking, and cursing; yet if he gives false weight and value to material appearance, he will still be an unspiritual person.

Spirit sees no obstruction or delays

Another aspect of the thinking of **Spirit** is that **Spirit** sees **no obstruction** and **no delays** in the completion of its plans. Man becomes a spiritual thinker when he aligns his thinking with this attitude. The average person gets a desire, sees a goal, wishes for a result; then, even as he is caught up in happy anticipation, the negative appears. Across his line of vision float menacing obstructions, doubts, and reasons why this thing he desires might not come true.

One characteristic difference between the earthy thinker and the spiritual thinker is this: while the former is thinking up all the reasons why a desire cannot come true, the latter is assembling all the **reasons why it can come true.**

Spirit lives in the eternal **Now.** Man lives in a world of time and space. With **Spirit,** to envisage a thing is to cause it to be created. Instantly, it is done. Man falsely sees his desire as something to be achieved or "demonstrated" at some later date; consequently, the thinking of many is unlike that of **Spirit** and is, therefore, unspiritual.

— Spirit sees the end from the beginning

In the last lesson, we said that at the moment of conception the whole man lies already in that fertilized ovum. He is not yet formed in all or any of his parts, but he is seen by **Spirit** as final and complete. In like manner, our demonstration is seen by **Spirit** as in final form **at the moment we conceive it.** Yesterday, today, and forever are as one moment to **Spirit,** living in the eternal **Now,** for **Spirit** thinks not in terms of time, process, development, or manufacture; it says, "Let there be . . . and there was."

MIND CARRIES OUT THE CREATIVE PROCESS

Spirit leaves all process, manufacture, evolving, and development to **Infinite Mind**, the working side of the **Trinity**. This the practitioner must also learn to do, for, when he thinks of obstruction and delay, he is thinking unspiritually. He must learn to say, "Let there be, and it **is** so."

To repeat from an earlier lesson: when one's desire is born, every channel for its fulfillment is immediately opened. The only thing that can close those channels is our belief in obstruction and delay.

CONSCIOUSNESS OF OMNIPOTENCE — ALL POWER

To develop the **consciousness** in the direction of **no obstruction or delay,** spend time contemplating the inner meaning of **Omnipotence** — not just a lot of power, but **All Power.** There is no opposing, hostile power; there could not be; there cannot be. There is no obstructing power whatever except a false belief in obstruction.

During treatment, think up every reason why this desired experience should come forth. Recall successful healings or demonstrations that you have heard about or read about or know first-hand. Dwell on the reasonableness of believing that **Omnipotence** can never be delayed. Think how, under the intelligent handling of the **Omnipotent,** the huge mass of suns and stars has never been able to delay its movement one second; the Niagara River cannot hold back from the Falls; fifty-story buildings are held close to the spinning earth by **Intelligence** acting as, and called by the name of gravity.

One student reported that he developed a tremendous sense of authority growing out of his awareness of **Omnipotence** that he acquired in this way:

Quietly he thought of all the power being generated by the automobiles on the single boulevard on which his office is located — millions of horsepower rolling by easily, effortlessly, every day. Then he thought of all the power of all the cars on all the highways of the world, of all the tractors on all the farms, the steam shovels, the machinery in all the factories, the motor power of all the airplanes, the ocean liners, the steam trains, the Diesel trucks, and the surges of electric power all over the globe until he was awed by the tremendous output of power through the hands of man.

He told himself, "The imposing might of all the earth's motors compared with **Omnipotence** is as the power of an ant compared

171

with that of an elephant.'' (Of course, this analogy is weak and imperfect because one cannot measure **Omnipotence**. It is beyond a quintillion units of power as represented by this comparative weighing of power as seen in ant and elephant.)

Finally, our student thought, ''All this **Power** flows through my word when I speak it for myself or for some other person. Nothing on earth can stop or obstruct it; nothing in heaven wishes to stop or obstruct it. It is done unto me now, at this moment, as I believe.''

These are only a few of the ways in which each person can develop his **consciousness** of this and other attributes of the **Infinite**. There are scores of other ways.

FINAL WORD AND BLESSING

In conclusion, I would encourage you, the student, by saying that the moment you ordered this course you started currents of mental and spiritual energy flowing that are continuing to operate within you whether you are conscious of them or not.

You are making greater progress than you know. People in this work always do. Sometimes they become discouraged because they constantly see loftier heights that their feet have not yet trod. The very seeing of the heights is an evidence of growth. Very often it takes others to call attention to the difference now showing in them.

The spiritual person is always much more spiritual than he realizes. His discontent with his ''unspirituality'' is an evidence of spirituality. His desire, plus his study, sets up a spiritualizing process deep within him, and as this is not seen on the surface, he usually does not know that it is going on; but there is a constant, steady purification of the soul that surrenders to these ideas. He can depend on this.

There is a beautiful hymn sung in some churches that begins:

> Take time to be holy;
>
> Speak oft with thy soul.

This the student must do. **Consciousness** grows wherever and whenever the student communes often with his innermost self, for in every man, as there has been in all the loftiest thinkers of all times, is that place where **spirit** with **Spirit** can meet. In the silences of one's thinking he comes close to God, and in that mystical meeting is communion; out of communion comes understanding; out of understanding comes power; and out of power come results.

> Let us not be weary in well doing, for in due season we shall reap if we faint not.

SPECIAL HELPS IN STUDY
AND PRACTICAL APPLICATION

These special helps have been carefully prepared to help you get the most out of this course.

Questions on the lesson

I advise that you first study the lesson carefully, then put it aside, write the answers to the questions, and, finally, **check your answers by the lesson.**

Keep the answers as a running commentary on the course **for your own benefit.** At its conclusion, you will find they have become a record of your own growth in consciousness.

1. What are some definite statements you can make about consciousness?

2. In clearing the pathway for the development of a high consciousness, what are some attitudes that must be removed from the thought?

3. In proportion to what does man's consciousness rise?

4. What are some steps in building a high consciousness?

5. How does **Spirit** view the universe?

6. What do we mean by "spiritual thinking"?

7. How does the attitude of the unspiritually minded person differ from that of **Spirit** in regard to completion of desires?

8. What are the respective places of **Spirit** and of **Mind** in the **Creative Process?**

9. How can one develop consciousness of **Omnipotence?**

10. If one does not progress as fast as he would like, what attitude should he take?

Collateral reading suggestions

Edith Armstrong: "Help Yourself"

Frederick Bailes: Your Mind Can Heal You, Chs. VII & X

Ernest Holmes (ed.): Mind Remakes Your World

Ervin Seale: Ten Words That Will Change Your Life

Practical application

. . . thought-training

As you meet in your daily associations or see as you walk down the street people who are ill or have physical malformations, or have defects of character and personality, or are undergoing some financial difficulty, practice looking right through the outer appearance to the perfect self within.

In doing so, you are developing your own healing consciousness and helping them at the same time.

. . . writing suggestion

Now that you have come to the end of this course, look back over the past weeks and set down a record of your progress.

In the first lesson, I suggested that you list the changes that you would like to come about in your life and also the changes in thought that you should make.

If you have exceeded the mark that you set for yourself, be very grateful that you have been able to do so; if you have fallen short, do not be discouraged. Good seed always grows.

. . . treatment for general good

This day I face toward the dawn of the **Infinite Healing Presence.**

I recognize it, like the sun coming over the hills, in an evergrowing sense of warmth, light, and life.

As I share the sun's rays by placing myself where they can play freely upon me, so I now place myself in the attitude of receptiveness to the **Infinite Healing Presence,** whose activity I welcome.

I bathe my consciousness in its steady, serene, healing rays.

I relinquish all personal struggle and effort, allowing myself to be played upon by that which is bringing healing and fulfillment in its invisible rays.

And it **is** so.

EXAMINATION

Within these pages is a set of questions by which you can test yourself on your understanding of this course.

I recommend that you review the twelve lessons very carefully. Some students will want to spend even more time on them before examining themselves.

When you are sure you are ready, select a time free of interruption.

Put aside all books and papers except the question sheet and the paper on which you will be writing.

Use paper that you can keep in your notebook.

There is no time limit.

After you have completed the examination, correct your answers by the course as you did for each of the twelve lessons.

To simplify your correcting of your answers, please note:

The questions are arranged in the same order as the answers appear in their most specific and longest form in the course.

Shorter answers and related ideas are throughout the course.

Keep your answers in your notebook for your future reference.

EXAMINATION QUESTIONS

Write fully, comprehensively, explicitly, on each of the questions.

Imagine you are doing this for someone who knows nothing about the Science of Mind but whom you would very much like to know about it, and you will find yourself writing in the clearest way possible.

1. Explain why we prefer to use the term "heal" rather than "cure."

2. Explain why our thought has power.

3. Why does **Power flow to the focus of attention,** and what is the significance of this?

4. Explain fully and clearly the **Creative Process** in the **Infinite** and in man, using a chart or charts, comparisons, and all means possible for absolute clarity.

5. How can we gain a sense of authority in treatment?

6. What is a treatment?

7. List and comment on at least five practical points in treatment.

8. Write a treatment for yourself or another person for any condition using any method.

9. What is the significance for us in our lives at all times and in treatment specifically that **Infinite Mind** is the **Knower?**

10. What does a healing consciousness mean to you, and how can one proceed definitely to cultivate it?

THOUGHTS FROM DR. BAILES' WRITINGS

The Science of Mind philosophy is not a few psychological tricks; it is a life to be lived.

*

The central core of the Science of Mind teaching is that there is a **Power** within every man, constantly available, that can lift his life to higher levels — from illness, defeat, and frustration into health, mastery, and success.

*

Right at the place where life seems hard is the **Power** to make it easy. Right in the middle of the deepest discouragement is the place where hope springs eternal. He who has decision of character, who stops his flight, who turns and faces life where it is hardest, steps immediately into the charmed circle of his **Divine** heritage.

*

Life is always for us, never against us; we are against ourselves unknowingly. Man was never intended to live a beaten, discouraged, or ill life; he was made for the very best of health and happiness.

*

Life is a mirror; it can reflect only that which is placed in front of it. If we want peace in the world, in the nation, in our relations with others, we can never get it by presenting a face distorted by rage, anxiety, hatred, envy, jealousy, or criticism.

*

Healing comes by a recognition of the fact that the **Power** that built the body did not immediately lose all interest in it. It has as much interest now as when it carefully built and assembled it cell by cell.

*

When the fear of the condition outweighs the knowledge of the **Power,** one cannot be healed. When the knowledge of the **Power** outweighs the fear of the condition, one can be healed.

*

Sensitiveness and self-pity are signs of emotional immaturity. The slave of self-pity is of all men most miserable because he need never take more than a few steps beyond his front door to find someone giving him a look or a word which confirms his false belief that the world is against him.

*

Love is the one great irresistible force of the universe, which sweeps away seeming obstacles and brings health, happiness, and prosperity to every single soul which opens itself up to its inflow.

*

When we give thanks for what we do not have, we are giving substance to things hoped for, evidence to things not seen.

*

God can be found in the beauty of a sunset, in the petals of a flower, in the planting of a garden, or in the laughter of children.

*

Man lives within his physical body for a few short years, but he is not the body; he is the never-dying thread of **Eternity,** stamped with an immortal life that had no beginning and shall have no ending.

EXTENDING THE BENEFITS

Many of you began treating for family and friends at once on beginning your study of this course. Others did so on my suggestion at the end of Lesson 8.

Now I am making a further suggestion: that you treat regularly for the raising of the consciousness of all students of this course with the resulting solution of their problems and the fulfillment of their most cherished desires. At the same time, you will be receiving the benefits of their treatment for you. This can be a very important and valuable outcome of your taking this course.

In the lessons on treatment, we found that a practical point is the naming of the person for whom the treatment is given. This is to make it definite in the mind of the practitioner; but **Infinite Mind,** carrying all knowledge within itself, knows who and where each person is. Not knowing the names of your fellow-students is, therefore, no hindrance to your giving effective treatment for them.

I am making another suggestion also, this one to follow up what I said in the Introduction about the impact of the thought of thousands of students on the world. My suggestion is that you treat regularly for all people. The following is a guide:

I know there is but **One Source.**

All men have come from that same **Source.**

We are all brothers whatever our nation, race, language, religion, or other particular beliefs.

We are all human beings first, and members of some particular group only secondarily.

We all have the same inner aspirations.

As I have come to see these fundamentals, so all men have it within themselves to see this great truth through the **Knower** within.

Infinite Mind, which surrounds us all and is in us all, is now revealing ourselves to ourselves so we see that the way of harmony and co-operation will bring well-being to the family of man.

I know that this consciousness is now becoming the consciousness of all men everywhere.

The **Law** of **Harmony** is all powerful.

I release this word to **Infinite Mind,** giving thanks that it **is** so.

BOOKS BY DR. BAILES

American Publishers

Hidden Power for Human Problems

    Prentice-Hall
    Englewood Cliffs, New Jersey 07632

Collected Essays of Frederick Bailes

Your Mind Can Heal You

The Healing Power of Balanced Emotions

Basic Principles of the Science of Mind:
    A Home Study Course (1971 revision)

    DeVorss & Company
    Marina del Rey, California 90294

Booklets:

Getting What You Go After

Healing the "Incurable"

Help Answer Your Own Prayers

How to Get Along with Troublesome People

Is There a Cure for Frustration?

The Secret of Healing

What Is This Power That Heals?

Your Emotions Can Kill or Cure

    DeVorss & Company
    Marina del Rey, California 90294

Please write for current price list to: DeVorss & Company,
P.O. Box 550, Marina del Rey, California 90294

BOOKS BY DR. BAILES

Foreign Publishers

Hidden Power for Human Problems
Your Mind Can Heal You

      Allen & Unwin
      40 Museum Street
      London WC1A 1LU. England

The Healing Power of Balanced Emotions
    (La Guérison par la Maîtrise des Sentiments)
Science of Mind Home Study Course
    (Santé, Prospérité, Sérénité)
Your Mind Can Heal You
    (Votre Esprit Peut Vous Guérir)

      Éditions d'Angles S.A.
      B. P. No. 36
      F-45800 Saint-Jean-de-Braye, France

Your Mind Can Heal You
    (Uw Denken Kan U Genezen)

      Uitgave Succes
      Prinsevinkenpark 2
      The Hague. Holland

Hidden Power for Human Problems
    (Shinnen — Kohfuku ne Seikatsu o umu Chikara)
Your Mind Can Heal You
    (Seishinryoku No Majutsu)

      Diamond Sha
      Diamond Building 3-3
      Kasumigaseki
      Chiyoda
      Tokyo. Japan

Hidden Power for Human Problems
    (Poder Oculto para Problemas Humanos)

      Editorial Diana, S. A.
      Roberto Gayol 1219
      Esquina Tlacoquemécatl
      Mexico 12, D. F.